C000217450

# the yacht
# owner's
# manual

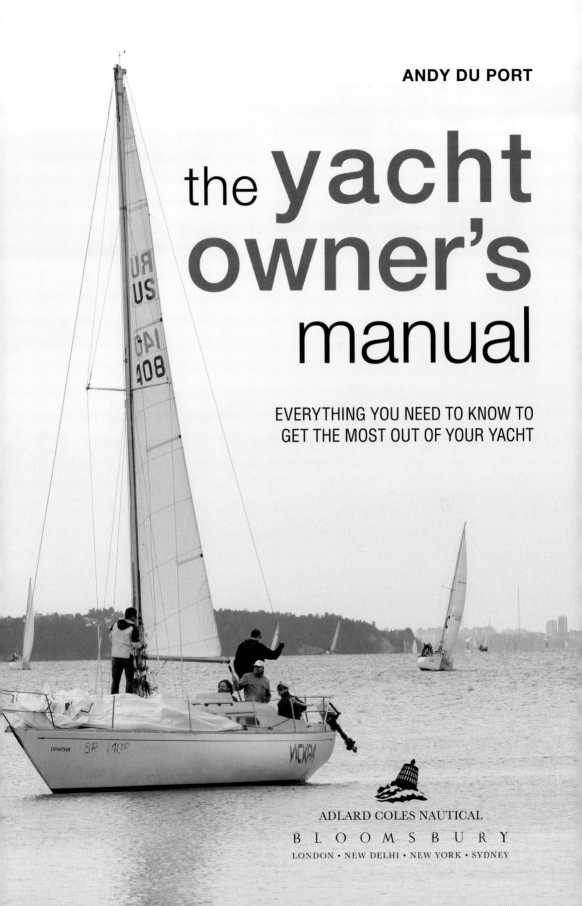

ANDY DU PORT

# the yacht owner's manual

## EVERYTHING YOU NEED TO KNOW TO GET THE MOST OUT OF YOUR YACHT

ADLARD COLES NAUTICAL

BLOOMSBURY

LONDON · NEW DELHI · NEW YORK · SYDNEY

**Adlard Coles Nautical**
An imprint of Bloomsbury Publishing Plc

50 Bedford Square
London
WC1B 3DP
UK

1385 Broadway
New York
NY 10018
USA

**www.bloomsbury.com**

**Adlard Coles, Adlard Coles Nautical and the Buoy logo are trademarks
of Bloomsbury Publishing Plc**

First published 2015

© Andy Du Port 2015

All images © of the author with the exception of the following which
are from Shutterstock: 2–3, 4–5, 6, 12, 20, 21, 23, 24, 32, 40 bottom,
56, 68, 76, 85, 90, 98, 101, 105, 110, 119, 121, 122, 128–9, 143

Cover photographs: front © David Harding, back © Shutterstock

Andy Du Port has asserted his right under the Copyright, Designs and Patents Act,
1988, to be identified as Author of this work.

All rights reserved. No part of this publication may be reproduced or transmitted
in any form or by any means, electronic or mechanical, including photocopying,
recording, or any information storage or retrieval system, without prior permission
in writing from the publishers.

No responsibility for loss caused to any individual or organization acting on or
refraining from action as a result of the material in this publication can be accepted
by Bloomsbury or the author.

**British Library Cataloguing-in-Publication Data**
A catalogue record for this book is available from the British Library.

| ISBN: | PB: | 978-1-4729-0548-2 |
|---|---|---|
|  | ePDF: | 978-1-4729-1390-6 |
|  | ePub: | 978-1-4729-1391-3 |

10 9 8 7 6 5 4 3 2 1

Typeset in 11/15pt URW Grotesk by Susan McIntyre
Printed and bound in China by RRD South China

To find out more about our authors and books visit
www.bloomsbury.com. Here you will find extracts,
author interviews, details of forthcoming events and
the option to sign up for our newsletters.

# CONTENTS

# INTRODUCTION

This book is aimed at the reasonably knowledgeable and experienced yachtsman or woman who is relatively new to yacht ownership, but I hope that it will also prove useful to those who have owned yachts for many years. It is not a sailing primer, nor will it attempt to provide you with absolutely everything you need to know about owning and caring for your yacht. That would take many volumes and still not be complete.

There is nothing quite like having your very own yacht. You are entirely responsible for fitting out, maintaining and sailing her, and solely accountable for all aspects of safety. You do not have to answer to a sailing school, yacht charterer or other owner, nor are you able to rely on someone else to fix things when they go wrong. You, and you alone, are the boss. You are skipper, navigator, engineer, cook, plumber and much more.

Does this sound a bit daunting? Well, many thousands of yachtsmen and women have taken the plunge before you, and there is a plethora of advice and information available – just search online or glance at the bookshelves of any chandlery. The snag is that most of this advice is either massively detailed or buried in obscure sources that can take ages to unearth. Few books, if any, bring it all together in one slim volume aimed at those who do not need to go back to basics but who want some simple, practical guidance to get started. If you subsequently need to explore a particular aspect of ownership or maintenance more thoroughly, you may need to do more research or seek specialist advice.

*Reefing early will give you confidence as you get to know your new boat.*

Before owning my first yacht about 35 years ago, I had sailed dinghies and various other craft, mainly with the Royal Navy, gaining an 'Offshore Skipper' qualification, as the RYA Yachtmaster Offshore was then known. Since then I have bought and owned five yachts. Two of them were bought through brokers; the other three were private purchases. Each boat has marked a milestone in my sailing activities, usually related to a growing family, but it was the first, a leaky old 25-foot wooden sloop, that gave me the most pleasure. She was totally mine, and I was in command. She had a very small and tired petrol engine, no VHF radio or any other electronics, no proper galley or fridge, but she sailed like a dream. I cruised the Solent and English Channel in her for several years before I realised that I was spending more of my precious leave maintaining her than actually out on the water. The change to GRP was inevitable, and the buying process started again.

The next was a 'composite' Twister (GRP hull and wooden coachroof). Although slightly longer, in many ways she was similar to the first one: worn-out petrol engine, long keel, and a marvellously sea-kindly yacht. Both these boats taught me a lot about yacht ownership. I had little money to spare so I had to choose equipment carefully and could not afford to pay someone to do the routine maintenance. During the next 13 years I slowly and rather reluctantly bowed to the pressures of the 20th century and installed a VHF radio and a furling headsail. I even reinstalled

*A breezy day off the Needles. Perfect conditions for training your crew before venturing further afield.*

the gas system so that the gas bottle no longer lived in the cockpit locker next to the hot engine exhaust. Not only did I own the Twister for a long time, I also married and had children, and the boat was just too small for a family of four. And so the buying process started once again.

Two more boats followed, a Westerly Griffon (shorter but much more room) and a Hallberg-Rassy 29. The latter not only had a VHF radio, a fixed echo sounder and log, she even had a fridge and a very basic chart plotter. The downside was that we quickly became used to these modern luxuries, and so maintenance and costs inexorably increased in order to keep everything running. After a few years, with growing children and more ambitious cruising plans, the inevitable search began for something a bit larger and faster. The result was our present boat, a Hallberg-Rassy 34. She is perfect for our needs: solidly built, ample room, handles beautifully under sail and power, and gets us across the Channel a good two hours faster than any of her predecessors. We also moved into the 21st century – literally and metaphorically – with radar, chart plotter, two fixed GPS sets, fridge and a hot air heater.

Although many maintenance tasks in a fibreglass boat are now much less onerous than in the days of wood, paint and varnish, most of the business of yacht ownership has not changed. Rigging, sails and engines still need checking and servicing on a regular basis, you must still navigate carefully and avoid other ships,

*Sheltered waters, such as the Solent, provide splendid opportunities for cruising, racing or just pottering from harbour to harbour.*

and you must still keep your crew safe and happy. Indeed, a skipper/owner now has to have more technical knowledge as electronics pervade all aspects of boating. Expectations of standards of comfort have also increased dramatically. No longer will crews put up with a cold, damp yacht where sleeping bags on hard bunks is the norm, and standard fare is bacon butties and chocolate bars. They now demand warmth, duvets and good food. They also, quite reasonably, expect to be kept safe without taking undue risks – a result of an increasingly litigious society, no doubt, but also added pressure on the skipper.

I have often been asked, not least by my wife and children, why we don't sail in sunny climes in a charter boat rather than put up with Northern European weather. The answer (with which they usually agree) is that we get just as much enjoyment from owning boats as we do from sailing them. In your own boat you can sail when and where you want to, rather than making the most of a charter holiday. Or you can just sit on board, with a cup of tea in hand, and watch the world go by instead of fretting about moving on because that is what you have paid good money to do.

So, where to begin? First, I start with a discussion on what sort of boat will best meet your sailing activities and aspirations. After that I offer hints and tips on all aspects of yacht ownership including navigation, engine maintenance, etiquette, safety, rigging, cooking and anything else that you may find useful as an owner. Indeed, this book is as much about domestics as it is about sailing or navigation. In that respect I am indebted to my wife and daughters whose priorities tend to focus on comfort and good food.

When you venture abroad in your own boat, you will need to obtain and complete all the necessary paperwork. It gets a mention in this book, but you can find more advice on this and passage planning in *Your First Channel Crossing* published by Adlard Coles Nautical.

Throughout the book I have included 'Headmarks' – useful aiming points that help you along the way. These address such varied topics as barbecues and cakes, and snubbers and split pins. They are shown in blue tinted boxes.

Finally, a huge amount of amplifying information – navigation, weather, first aid, safety, tides, radio and much more – can be found in *Reeds Nautical Almanac* (referred to later as just *Reeds*). It is updated every year and I for one would never sail without a copy on board. It is also available in digital format for use on PCs and iPads.

*Arrive in good time to enjoy a peaceful evening in harbour.*

# CHOOSING YOUR YACHT

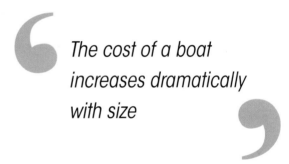

*The cost of a boat increases dramatically with size*

## WHICH YACHT IS BEST FOR YOU?

It is almost impossible to give definitive advice about which yacht will be the most suitable for you. It depends on so many factors: your sailing area, whether you cruise or race (or both), offshore or coastal, berthing arrangements and the needs of your family. The starting point, however, will almost always be your budget.

A glance at the brokerage pages of the yachting press will show that you can spend anything from a few thousand pounds to several million. Generally you get what you pay for, but not always. Like many things – cars, clothes, electrical goods – you often pay a premium for a brand name without much gain in quality or reliability. Many of the mass-produced yachts are excellent value compared with their classier equivalents. This applies to both new and second-hand, although some used boats hold their value so well that buying new is not much more expensive. Have a look at as many as possible, decide what suits you, then scour the market for a particular boat.

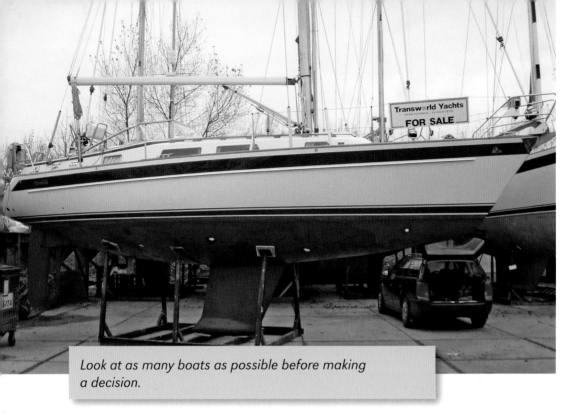

*Look at as many boats as possible before making a decision.*

In no particular order, let's consider some of the fundamentals:

## Size

The cost of a boat increases dramatically with size. There may seem to be little difference in size between, say, a 30-foot and 33-foot yacht of a particular make, but the cost will be much more. Is it worth it? Not only will the purchase price increase with size but so will berthing fees and maintenance. A typical South Coast marina may charge £450 per metre per year, so you are looking at significant savings by opting for the smaller boat. Visitors' berthing fees in most harbours are also charged by boat length, and these can mount up during a sailing season.

On the face of it, maintenance costs may not seem to be directly related to size but, again, lift-out fees are based on length, and the bigger the boat, the more materials you will need to keep her sound and smart. Antifouling paint is not cheap! The bigger the boat, the bigger the engine (probably), meaning more fuel and more expensive servicing bills.

It may be that you have particular requirements for accommodation, and thus the size of boat. For example, headroom below decks or wide side decks may be important to you. Older designs often provide berths in the saloon whereas modern boats tend to reserve this area for living and dining, thereby relegating useful bunk space to the forepeak and/or an after cabin. If you are planning to sail offshore for prolonged periods, look carefully at which bunks can be used at

*All shapes and sizes. Take time to choose the best boat for you.*

sea. Sleeping in the forepeak in rough weather can be like trying to relax in a spin drier. If you have a young family and are looking to the future, remember that small children may be happy to share a bunk, but when they get older they will almost certainly demand their own space.

Finally, a bigger boat will probably be more comfortable at sea and is likely to sail faster, but if your sailing is mainly in local waters, does this really matter?

## Keels

One keel or two? One keel will almost always provide better sailing qualities, but some bilge keel yachts sail surprisingly well and you may not have to sacrifice too much in this respect. The main disadvantage of a single keel is draft. Whether or not this is a consideration for you will depend on your area and sailing activities. In the Thames Estuary and on the East Coast, you can be quite restricted by depth – even the difference between a draft of 1.5m and 2m may determine whether you can enter many harbours at most states of the tide or only near high water. Also, while a fin keel boat may be easy to handle under power, a long keel will almost certainly mean that manoeuvring in tight spaces, especially when going astern, becomes much more difficult.

If you plan to dry out on sandy beaches, there is only one choice: a bilge-keeler. Even if you don't plan to take the ground, you may sleep better when the tide goes out.

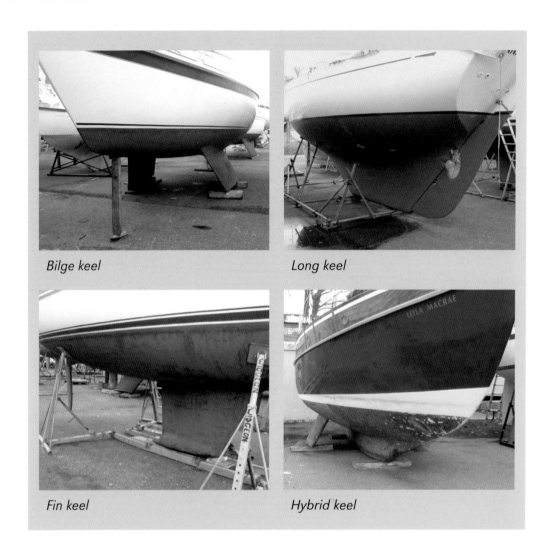

Bilge keel

Long keel

Fin keel

Hybrid keel

You can have what seems to be the best of both worlds by choosing a boat with a lifting keel. Not only do they sail well, they can also dry out. However, be aware that the keel housing and associated gear may take up quite a lot of valuable space in the saloon. Raising and lowering the keel may require considerable muscle power and time. Maintenance can also be a problem.

## Wheel or tiller

If you buy a yacht with a centre cockpit, you will have a wheel. Even if the cockpit is aft many yachts are now fitted with a wheel as standard. Think carefully about this as the design of the rudder stock may allow for simple conversion to tiller steering. The advantages of a tiller over a wheel are almost too many to mention. Here are just a few:

# ADVANTAGES OF A TILLER

### ■ Space in the cockpit

A wheel takes up a huge amount of room in a small cockpit, and this is where you spend much of your time while living on board. Chatting to your friends through the spokes of a wheel is not ideal and there is little space for a cockpit table, limiting your options for al fresco dining. A tiller can be hinged so that it is well out of the way.

### ■ The 'feel' for the boat when sailing

A wheel provides little feedback from the rudder, so weather helm, for example, may be hard to detect. If the boat is not well balanced, more helm will be required to keep her on course, and the slower you will sail.

### ■ Access to winches etc

Some boats are well laid out in this respect but in many you may find yourself trapped behind the wheel, not easily able to reach the sheet winches or even the mainsheet. If the halyards and reefing lines are led aft to the cockpit, you are unlikely to be able to reach them either from behind the wheel. This may not be significant in a fully crewed yacht, but it certainly is if you are short-handed or find yourself alone in the cockpit trying to trim the sails.

### ■ Space below the cockpit

In some yachts the linkages between the wheel and the rudder are immediately below the cockpit sole and encroach into the aft cabin. My present boat came with a wheel, and when I removed it to install a tiller I freed up about 9 inches of headroom above the after bunks.

### ■ Simplicity

A tiller is connected directly to the rudder stock so there is nothing 'mechanical' to go wrong. A wheel is mounted on a pedestal and connected via wires, rods, chains or hydraulics to a quadrant on the stock. Not only is there plenty to go wrong, but even in the best systems there is a lot of friction, hence the lack of feel.

An autopilot connected to a tiller, invaluable when sailing short-handed, is usually much simpler and less costly than one designed for a wheel. At the most basic level, but still perfectly adequate, some have their own built-in compass, and only require a power source rather than an additional connection to a fixed fluxgate (or similar) compass. Again, less to go wrong.

### ■ Quick reaction

To take immediate avoiding action, you can move a tiller from one side to the other almost instantly; a wheel takes much longer. You also know exactly where the rudder is 'pointing'; with a wheel it is far from obvious.

### ■ Shelter

A wheel is usually mounted well aft, leaving the helmsman exposed to the weather. With a tiller of suitable length, you are able to move forward and find some protection from the spray hood.

*A tiller can be folded out of the way, leaving plenty of room in the cockpit.*

*In this identical boat the wheel is taking up a lot of space.*

Nevertheless, there are some advantages in having a wheel:

## ADVANTAGES OF A WHEEL

■ **Familiarity**
Some people like the similarity with a car's steering wheel.

■ **Comfort**
Steering while facing forward can be more comfortable than sitting athwartships.

■ **Visibility**
It can be easier to sit well to one side while steering with one hand (although a tiller extension may be just as effective).

■ **Controls**
Engine controls are normally mounted on the steering pedestal making them easier to operate. Similarly, the steering compass and other instruments are likely to be closer to the helmsman – but perhaps not so accessible to the skipper/navigator.

None of the above outweighs, to my mind, the advantages of tiller steering. Some people will argue that a large yacht must have a wheel just because of her size. I don't agree. For many years I sailed an old 55-foot wooden yacht with a tiller with no problems. That said, you will be hard-pressed now to find a modern yacht over about 36 feet that is not fitted with a wheel as standard.

# FINDING THE BOAT

Let us now assume that you have settled on the type and size of boat you want to buy, and that you have perhaps even decided on a particular make/model. What next? Do you go to a broker or buy privately? As usual, there is no clear answer. A broker will cost more (the seller pays the broker but this will obviously be reflected in the asking price), but you will have the full support of a professional, just like you get from an estate agent when buying a house. It is, of course, perfectly feasible to buy privately (I have on several occasions) but you need to take advice on what paperwork needs to be completed and signed to make the whole transaction legal and binding. It is not overly complicated. The bill of sale is the most important document. It shows who you bought the boat from and for how much. It also identifies you as the new owner. Further advice may be obtained from the Royal Yachting Association (RYA) at www.rya.org.uk.

Before this you must find the boat. There are myriad online sites and lots of brokerage pages in the yachting press. Clearly it is much easier if you know exactly what you want, and it is convenient if the boat of your dreams is located somewhere near you. If you live or sail on the South Coast, you will probably be spoilt for choice. Whatever you do, look at as many boats as possible. By doing this you will get a feel for what is available and the current market prices.

When you view a boat, have a really good poke around. You will soon see whether she has been well cared for and if the owner has

### ■ Equipment

Most used yachts will be sold with a good inventory, but beware of the 'extras' if buying new. Even basic kit such as instruments, anchors, warps and fenders may not be included in the price, and you certainly won't get a dinghy, liferaft or cutlery and crockery. Study the inventory carefully and be sure that all items listed are actually included in the sale and that they are in working order.

### ■ Owners' associations

This may not be an important factor in choosing a yacht, but bear in mind that some classes have owners' associations that not only provide useful information and support to their members, but also arrange rallies, talks and other activities that can help you to get the best out of your boat while enjoying the company of other like-minded yotties.

### ■ Berthing arrangements

Very small yachts may be kept ashore and launched by trailer. However, most will be berthed in marinas or on swinging moorings. The latter is the less expensive option, but you will need a suitably seaworthy boat to transfer you, your crew and gear to and from the shore. Such a boat may be too large to double up as the yacht's tender.

prepared her properly for sale. A musty smell, a grubby galley or lots of unstowed gear indicate that the boat has not been loved.

The distance between home and a potential new boat is not necessarily an insurmountable problem. I once bought a boat in Inverness even though I live on the South Coast and my home port is Gosport. Yes, I had to fork out for the air fare to go and inspect her, but I got the boat I wanted for very little extra expense. I then had to get her from the Moray Firth to the Solent, but she had so much spare gear on board (the owner was giving up sailing altogether) that it was impossible to sail her down. With a bit of research and negotiation I found a boat transport firm that delivered her right to my sailing club for little more than the overall expense (travel, marina dues, food, crew etc) of sailing her south myself.

## Survey

Your insurer may demand a survey, but this will depend on the make, construction and age of the vessel. Even if there is no requirement for a full survey, you would be well advised to ask a professional surveyor or other experienced person to have a good look. If the hull is GRP, a set of moisture readings below the waterline is well worth the expense – for peace of mind, if nothing else. Osmosis on younger boats is now mercifully rare, but very costly to put right. If you are lucky, the previous owner may let you have sight of a recent survey, which will, as a minimum, give you an idea of the overall state of the boat at the time of the survey.

*A classic yacht with a long keel will sail well but might be tricky to manoeuvre under power.*

*A boat will need to be ashore if you are having a full hull survey.*

Common sense comes into play here. Look at everything and don't be afraid to ask questions. Has she been used for racing (possibly more wear and tear than a cruising boat)? Has she been laid up ashore during the winter (giving the hull time to dry out)? How old are the sails? When was the standing rigging last renewed? Has she suffered any damage? If so, was it professionally repaired (see the receipts)? When was the engine last serviced? Make a note of the answers to these and all the other questions that spring to mind. A powerful torch, a mirror (for looking into awkward places) and a notebook are invaluable aids to a self-survey.

*Be Your Own Boat Surveyor*, published by Adlard Coles Nautical, is helpful in giving pointers about what to look out for before engaging a professional surveyor, and could save you paying for numerous surveys on boats that you could have already judged to be unsuitable or in poor condition.

Most professional surveys don't include the engine, so you may need to seek a marine engineer's advice. Evidence of regular servicing and a log of engine hours will help, but there is no substitute for getting underway and seeing, and hearing, the engine running. Be very wary of difficult starting from cold, evidence of black smoke or odd noises. We all rely on our engine at times, and replacing one can incur more expense than the rest of the yacht is worth.

# MAKING AN OFFER

Once you have made the decision to buy you need to make an offer, just as you would when buying a house. Very few sellers expect to get what they ask for, and by this time you may have a feel for how keen the current owner is to reach a deal. Perhaps he/she is already in the process of buying another boat, and is therefore anxious to complete the sale quickly. If the seller is giving up sailing, you may be in a good position to negotiate the inclusion of spare gear, winter covers, even crockery and cutlery at no extra cost. As I have already mentioned, this happened to me a few years ago and I managed to persuade the owner to part with nearly the entire contents of his garage, which was almost full of boat gear.

It doesn't matter whether you are making a private purchase or using a broker. The only difference is that you may be more comfortable negotiating through a third party rather than face-to-face. Indeed, a good broker should be able to advise you about a realistic bid for the owner to consider. However, a broker makes his money by charging a percentage of the final price, so he is unlikely to haggle too hard on your behalf.

There is some difference of opinion as to whether the result of the survey can be used as a bargaining tool. In general terms, if you have agreed to buy 'subject to survey' only an unforeseen disaster would allow you to pull out altogether. To guard against this, you might be asked for a deposit, which would only be returnable in the event of an unexpectedly poor survey. Be very clear on this before you make your offer. On the other hand, relatively minor items picked up during a survey, which were not readily apparent beforehand, might permit you to further negotiate the final price. Some prospective owners have a survey conducted before even making an offer. This could be expensive, but may put you in a good position if there is a significant amount of work to be done to bring her up to a sensibly seaworthy condition.

Now comes the painful bit: paying. A private seller may accept a personal cheque, but more likely – and almost certainly if you are paying a broker – you will need to arrange for a bank draft or other guaranteed payment method.

# TAKING POSSESSION

The final step is to board your yacht and sail her away! She won't legally be yours until the payment has been accepted and a bill of sale signed. Normally there is no problem with this, but don't be tempted to short-cut the system. Not only might

*Be sure to have an experienced crew on board for your first few trips.*

your insurance be invalid if you get underway before the paperwork is complete, you could even wind up in court.

Unless you are taking over the previous owner's mooring or berth, you will need to move the boat soon after becoming her new owner. Take your time to plan your first trip, and muster a sufficiently experienced crew to help you. However eager they may be, this is probably not a good time to embark the entire family. I fell into that trap once, and our then three-year-old daughter insisted on 'having a go' on the helm within minutes of leaving the berth. To avoid a toddler temper tantrum, I let her have her way but was quite relieved when she got bored after a few minutes.

3

# PAPERWORK

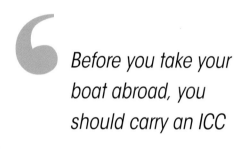

*Before you take your boat abroad, you should carry an ICC*

You have had the fun of choosing your yacht and you have done all the form-filling associated with the purchase, but of course the paperwork doesn't end there. Now you need to address other official and unofficial paperwork. Although the previous owner should be able to produce most of the following, much of it will have to be put into your name as the new owner.

## FORMAL PAPERWORK

### Insurance

Unlike a car, there is no legal requirement for a yacht to be insured. However, most, if not all, marinas and harbour authorities, at home and abroad, insist that craft using their facilities must have at least third-party insurance. Shop around for the best deal, making sure you are covered for your particular needs. In other words, read the small print rather than opting for the cheapest quote.

Check that the geographical sailing area is clearly stated and that you are covered, if appropriate, for racing. If you intend to sail by yourself, be wary of the precise wording of the policy. Some insurers will provide cover only for 'dawn to dusk' or 'daylight' (whatever that means). Others are more precise and state 'sunrise to sunset'. My insurer allows me to sail single-handed for up to 18 consecutive hours, which is sensible and unequivocal. Whatever the wording, you will almost certainly have to agree to a larger excess in the event of a claim when either racing or sailing by yourself.

## Registration

Although it is not a legal requirement to register your boat if sailing in UK waters, you are very strongly recommended to do so before going abroad. Registration on Part I of the UK Ship Register enables you to prove title to your boat; prove her nationality; use the boat as security to obtain a marine mortgage; and obtain 'Transcripts of Registry', which show the yacht's previous owners and whether there are any outstanding mortgages. In 2014, registration on Part I cost £124 and this is renewable every five years.

The cheaper, and much more usual, option is to be registered on Part III, the Small Ships Register (SSR). This is relatively inexpensive (£25 for five years) and is equally valid in the eyes of officialdom. It shows your SSR number and boat details, including the Hull Identification (HID) number and the registered owner, but it is not proof of ownership. You can register online at www.mcga.gov.uk. You will find further advice from the RYA.

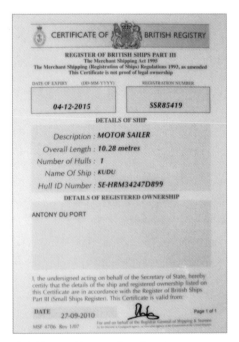

A SSR certificate showing boat details and the registered owner.

## Proof of VAT status

You may only use a boat within the EU if she is VAT paid or deemed to be VAT paid. VAT will normally be paid when bought from new or, if imported from outside the EU, when the vessel is imported to the UK.

One exception is for boats that were in use as private pleasure craft prior to 1 January 1985, and that were in the EU on 31 December 1992. They are deemed to be VAT paid under EU single-market transitional arrangements. If your boat falls into this category, you will need to be

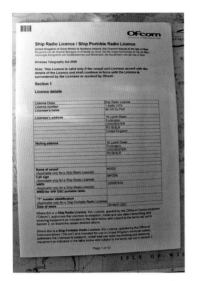

*A Ship Radio Licence must be carried on board at all times.*

able to prove her age (builder's certificate) and that she was in the EU (marina receipts, survey report etc).

The rules are quite complicated, and more details can be found from HM Revenue and Customs at www.hmrc.gov.uk (search for 'notice 8'). Not being able to prove that VAT has been paid could land you with a very large bill.

## Ship Radio Licence

If you have a radio on board, it is a legal requirement to have a Ship Radio Licence and, in the wording of the licence itself, it 'shall be kept with or near to the licensed radio equipment at all times, where it is physically practicable to do so'. All radio equipment carried on board is listed on the licence, and it will show the vessel's call sign and Maritime Mobile Service Identity (MMSI) number for DSC radios. It is an offence to use any radio equipment not covered by a Ship Radio Licence. Once obtained, it is valid for life unless surrendered by you or revoked by Ofcom (www.ofcom.org.uk). You also need an Authority to Operate (see below).

## VHF Licence (Authority to Operate)

Before the radio is used someone on board must hold an 'Authority to Operate'. This will normally be a Short Range Certificate (SRC) for VHF/DSC, which is personal to the individual, and it must be carried on board. Courses are available at RYA training centres, and many clubs run their own courses on behalf of the RYA. This does not mean that only the licence holder may operate the radio. So long as someone on board holds a licence, any crew member may use the radio with the express permission of the licence holder, who remains responsible for all transmissions.

*A Short Range Certificate covers the needs of most yacht skippers.*

On inland waters your VHF radio may also need to be ATIS (Automatic Transmitter Identification System) capable, but this doesn't apply on, for example, the canal between Ouistreham and Caen. Again, the RYA can provide more details.

## Recreational Craft Directive (RCD) – Declaration of Conformity

This only applies to vessels built after 16 June 1998. If for some reason you don't hold a Declaration of Conformity, you will need to contact the builder to obtain one. The penalties for not being able to produce one are severe. If your boat was built before 16 June 1998, you should be able to provide proof, perhaps a builder's certificate or mooring receipts, that she was in existence before that date.

## International Certificate of Competence (ICC)

Before you take your boat abroad, you should carry an ICC (which may be obtained by application to the RYA) and any other proof of competence, such as RYA qualifications. If you are intending to venture inland, an ICC valid for 'Inland Waters' must be carried along with a copy of the CEVNI (**C**ode **E**uropéen des **V**oies de la **N**avigation **I**ntérieure) rules. To get this endorsement you will have to pass the CEVNI test.

*It is wise to carry an ICC when cruising abroad.*

# INFORMAL PAPERWORK

Of the less formal paperwork, the following is worth considering.

## Red diesel receipts

These are not strictly necessary, but many EU countries are at odds with the UK's concession that allows recreational craft to purchase red 'duty free' diesel. If you have red diesel in your tanks, keep all receipts showing where it was bought and how much duty was paid. A record of engine hours and fuel consumption will also help. Red diesel in cans is not normally permitted outside the UK and it is strongly recommended that any cans contain only white, duty-paid diesel such as you would buy from a garage ashore.

## Data book

You will at some time need to fill in forms requiring your boat's overall length (or LOA), beam, draft, even tonnage. It is a good idea to have all this in one place, so I have made up a 'data book' containing all the come-in-handy information, which I can refer to at short notice. In addition to the boat's details, the book contains the following:

- Emergency procedures including MAYDAY and PAN PAN check-off lists

- MSI broadcasts including shipping and inshore forecast times and areas

- Waypoints list for rapid reference

- Wiring diagrams for batteries, engine and lighting circuits, and all the wires that go up the mast

- Fuel consumption table for calculating fuel remaining in the main tank

- International signal code flags/ Morse code

- Height of tide diagram and tidal curve for my own home port

- International Port Traffic Signals

- Diagram of running rigging. Eight ropes run from the foot of my mast to the cockpit so it is handy to know which is which when fitting out

- Leaving boat checks including locking up, turning off the gas, lowering flags, pumping bilges, turning off the battery switches and what to take home (car keys, phone, wallet etc). It is amazing what you forget!

Adlard Coles Nautical produces a *Maintenance Log* with handy pages for all the loose odds and ends (passwords, model numbers, service dates, wiring diagrams etc) to enable you to keep everything together in one place. Some owners use the back of their logbook for this.

## Log

There is no legal requirement to keep a log, but I think this is one of the most important documents in any vessel. Not only is it a narrative of what you have done and where you have been, it is also a navigational record and shows essential planning data, such as weather forecasts and tidal data, which might be needed in case of an accident.

You can buy formatted logbooks but I prefer to make up my own loose-leaf version, which is customised to my boat and my requirements (see next page for an example). It is cheap and simply a matter of printing more pages when (preferably before!) you run out.

## EXAMPLE LOG PAGES

### [Name of yacht]

**Date** ....................................................

**Time Zone:** Zulu / Alpha / Bravo

**From/At** ...............................................

**Towards** .........................................

**Crew** .............................................................................................................

| Engine hours (start) | ...................... | Fuel (start) | ................................ |
|---|---|---|---|
| Engine hours (today) | ...................... | Fuel used/(added) | ............................... |
| Total (since oil change) | ...................... | Fuel remaining | ............................... |

Log (end):

Log (start):          **Day's Run:**          M    **Time Underway:**          Hrs          Mins

| REMARKS | ENGINE | | |
|---|---|---|---|
|  | Start | Stop | Time |
|  |  |  |  |
|  |  |  |  |
|  |  |  |  |
|  |  |  |  |
|  |  |  |  |
|  |  |  |  |
|  |  |  |  |
|  |  |  |  |
|  |  |  |  |
|  |  |  |  |
|  |  |  |  |
|  |  |  |  |
|  |  |  |  |
|  |  |  |  |
|  |  |  |  |
|  |  |  |  |
|  |  |  |  |
|  |  |  |  |
|  |  |  |  |
|  |  |  |  |
|  |  |  |  |
|  |  |  |  |
| TOTAL | - | - |  |

# [Name of yacht]
## TIDES

Port .................................    Port .................................    Port ...............................

| | | |
|---|---|---|
| HW | HW | HW |
| LW | LW | LW |
| HW | HW | HW |
| LW | LW | LW |
| Range: | Range: | Range: |

Tidal Coefficient:        am              pm

**Weather Forecast** ............................................................................................
..............................................................................................................

| Time | Course (°M) | Log | Dist Run | Wind Dir Force | Baro | Position |
|---|---|---|---|---|---|---|
| 0000 | | | | | | |
| 0100 | | | | | | |
| 0200 | | | | | | |
| 0300 | | | | | | |
| 0400 | | | | | | |
| 0500 | | | | | | |
| 0600 | | | | | | |
| 0700 | | | | | | |
| 0800 | | | | | | |
| 0900 | | | | | | |
| 1000 | | | | | | |
| 1100 | | | | | | |
| 1200 | | | | | | |
| 1300 | | | | | | |
| 1400 | | | | | | |
| 1500 | | | | | | |
| 1600 | | | | | | |
| 1700 | | | | | | |
| 1800 | | | | | | |
| 1900 | | | | | | |
| 2000 | | | | | | |
| 2100 | | | | | | |
| 2200 | | | | | | |
| 2300 | | | | | | |
| 2400 | | | | | | |

# CREW

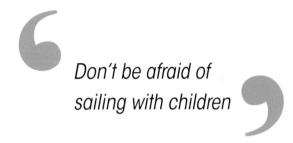

*Don't be afraid of sailing with children*

If you are already an experienced skipper, you will be familiar with the issues surrounding the selection of a crew and how to employ them effectively and safely. As a new owner, you may not often have sailed, if ever, with just your family. In this section I offer a few hints and tips on successful sailing with your nearest and dearest, focussing on the younger members. We then look at the experience and qualifications of the crew, depending on your intended boating activities.

As the skipper you must keep everyone safe and happy. The first is obvious, and if you fail in the second you face misery, mutiny or lots of single-handed sailing.

## CREW RULES

### Shouting

First, don't shout! There is nothing more guaranteed to put your family off sailing than you bellowing at them. To anyone within earshot it sounds as though you don't know what you are doing and creates a general air of uncertainty and inefficiency. Secondly, if you must raise your voice – and there are sometimes good reasons for doing so – try to use standard seagoing terminology. This may seem nit-picking in the extreme, but most people do use the correct terms and you will stick out like a

*Nearly at the end of a long passage - and a run ashore in sight!*

> *There is nothing more guaranteed to put your family off sailing than you bellowing at them*

sore thumb if you don't. I recently sailed in company with a new owner who was forever yelling 'Release the lines!' when leaving from alongside. Not only did no one know which lines he was referring to but 'Let go the bow line' would have been so much clearer. Once you have been sailing with a regular crew for some time, there is often no need to say anything. Brief them beforehand, then just use hand signals.

## Children

Don't be afraid of sailing with children. The earlier they start the better, but even if they are not introduced to sailing until in their teens there is no reason why they shouldn't enjoy the experience. There are a couple of golden rules: don't yell at them, and do allow them to take a full part in running the boat. Also, make it fun. You may want to thrash across the Channel in a force 6 in order to have a slap-up

# HAVING FUN!

An ex-RN friend of mine recently admitted that he had tried to run his first yacht like a warship: everything by the book and little tolerance for 'non-nautical' language or general frivolity. He quickly lost the goodwill of his wife and children and had to relax his ways before mutiny became a reality. (Actually, it did but that's another story.)

There are times when clear orders and willing obedience are necessary, and the sensible use of nautical terms will avoid confusion. However, most of us go sailing to enjoy ourselves in the company of others. The atmosphere you establish as skipper will soon be reflected by your crew – they will either continue sailing with you, or you will become very lonely.

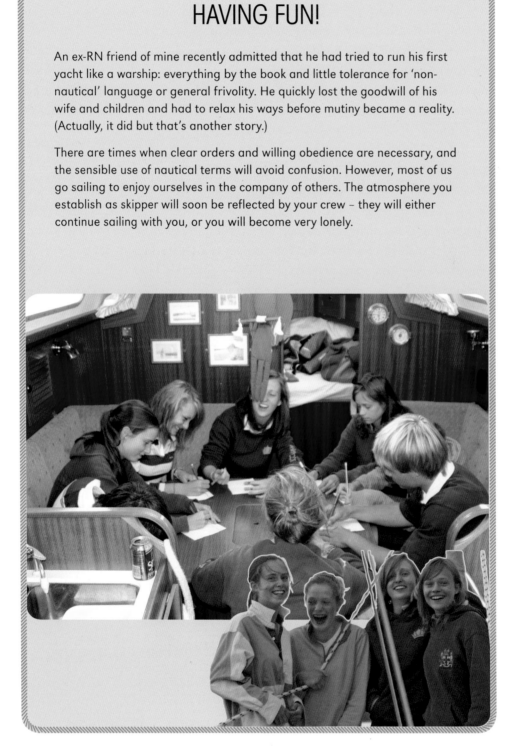

meal in Cherbourg accompanied by a few bottles of wine, but the children may be longing for a short hop to a sandy beach and a barbecue. Given time, they will probably relish some salty offshore sailing, but go easy to begin with.

I know one family whose teenage children were keen and eager to try yachting in a newly acquired boat. However, Dad didn't really know what he was doing and tended to panic and shout. His wife and children picked up on this and lost confidence. Within three years they had sold the boat. I'm surprised they stuck it out that long.

## Babies and toddlers

Babies on board are not a problem; ask any sailing parent. All they need is feeding, changing and regular cuddles. So long as you are around, they will be content. Later, at the toddler stage, things get rather more testing. They will be too small to take an active part in sailing the boat, but may expect to be entertained, although I don't know of any who won't amuse themselves if they are left to fend for themselves. Our two daughters became adept at inventing games and playing with their toys – yes, they have to come along too – before they were able to keep a lookout, steer and help with sheets, ropes and fenders. They both now hold RYA qualifications and still come sailing with us in their mid 20s. I suspect the lure of a free holiday may have something to do with it.

*A warm and happy crew – make sure they are suitably dressed for the conditions.*

*Even a strong wind can be safe and fun, but be aware of your crew's limitations.*

## Weather

I have already mentioned the fun of sailing. This does not mean that you should only sail in benign conditions, but you do need to judge the experience and stamina of your crew and heed their wishes. A fast and furious sail in an offshore gale can be huge fun in a well-found boat with a confident and sensible skipper. The same conditions can become a nightmare if the skipper is fretting and allowing his crew to become cold, wet and frightened. I was once sailing an RN yacht with a crew of very mixed experience on a cold, breezy November day. We had taken in a couple of reefs but there was salt water all over the place and the boat was lively, to say the least. When things calmed down I asked the least experienced member if he had been frightened. He replied, 'I was at first, then I saw that you weren't, so I wasn't!' Actually, I was somewhat concerned at times but I succeeded in not showing it.

Cards and board games are great for days like this!

A wet and windy sail may call for plenty of hot drinks and snacks.

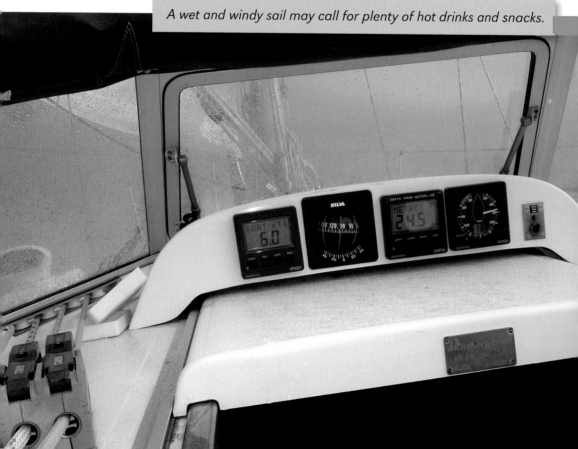

## Problems

That said, if things do start going wrong or conditions become more than you can manage, think about it, form a plan and then explain the situation clearly and calmly to the crew. This will help you to focus on the priorities and do your job of getting the boat to shelter safely, with the help and encouragement of a well-briefed and composed crew.

## Rules and regulations

Mercifully, we are not yet bound by any regulations concerning manning levels or qualifications for privately owned pleasure craft in the UK. If you want to sail by yourself or with a totally inexperienced crew, that is up to you – and you don't need to ask anyone's permission to do so. However, as usual, common sense comes into play. Ask

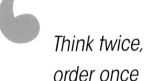

*Think twice, order once*

yourself what would happen if you were incapacitated for any reason. If you are singled-handed there aren't many options, but assuming there is at least one other person on board, they should know how to summon help and, ideally, be able to get you and the boat back to a safe harbour.

Qualifications don't tell the whole story, so beware of relying on them unless you also have a good idea of the person's experience as well. There are plenty of 'fast track' Yachtmasters who have almost no hands-on experience. Similarly, I know of many people who have no qualifications at all but are hugely experienced and with whom I would sail anywhere in any conditions. In the chapter on paperwork we mentioned the International Certificate of Competence (ICC). This is not a qualification in its own right but may be required by the authorities abroad. For a cross-Channel trip or equivalent, a Day Skipper and at least one Competent Crew would be a sensible minimum.

## Briefing the crew

We will look at safety procedures later in the book; for now I am suggesting that you select your crew according to your sailing plans. A quiet outing in sheltered local waters may require no more than a short safety brief (lifejackets, harnesses and other basic considerations) before setting off. A more adventurous trip requires an in-depth safety brief, and you should embark a crew that is up to the task. Specifically, appoint a mate who can play a full part in a crisis or take over if you are incapacitated.

*A new crew needs a thorough briefing before setting off.*

## Pets

Whether you regard your dog as a member of your crew is up to you, but you need to be aware of the regulations for taking pets abroad. As a rule of thumb, your dog (or cat or any other animal) may not be taken into any foreign port in

a private vessel even if they have been professionally checked and have their own 'passport'; they must travel on an approved carrier – a ferry or aircraft. This rule does not apply to the Channel Islands or Ireland, but don't take my word for it, check beforehand.

Also, be aware that even some UK harbours do not allow dogs on their pontoons or other harbour property. At the time of writing, Newlyn is a case in point.

*There is no reason why your pets should not enjoy sailing with you.*

# A GOOD SKIPPER

Crew morale doesn't depend only on safe sailing and a benevolent skipper. Comfort, food and other domestic considerations play their part. We will look at these in the next chapter. In the meantime, here is a short checklist of just some of the qualities of a good skipper:

- Keep calm and don't raise your voice unnecessarily. If you exude an air of relaxed professionalism your crew will soon settle down to enjoy their sailing in the knowledge that their skipper knows what he/she is doing.

- Think about the programme and sail well within your, and your crew's, capacity. Gain confidence with short, relatively undemanding trips before venturing further afield or tackling more challenging conditions. You will gain far more respect as skipper by being sensibly cautious rather than taking needless risks.

- Get into the habit of seeking the preferences of your crew and then briefing them thoroughly on the plan. Give them alternatives in case circumstances change. If everything goes well, your standing as a skipper will be enhanced. If not, at least they won't be taken by surprise.

- Plan the passage thoroughly. The less you have to do in this respect while underway, the more time you will have for sailing the boat and looking after the crew. While making your approach to your destination is not a good time to dart below to work out the height of tide or look up the correct VHF channel for contacting the harbour office.

- Obtain a weather forecast at every opportunity. Note the times in the log and remember to tune in in good time. This applies as much to a trip in local waters as to an extended offshore passage. Forewarned is forearmed, and a threatened change in the weather may enable you to modify your plan in plenty of time to avoid unpleasant conditions or an unseemly dash for shelter.

- Keep your crew informed of your progress and share your thoughts with them. If you are considering diverting to a port of refuge, talk it through and pool your collective expertise and experience. You make the decision, but you will be surprised how often your crew will be having the same ideas. They may be putting on a brave face, but they will be grateful if you ask 'Are we really enjoying this, or shall we call it a day?'

# DOMESTIC ISSUES

*Feed them well
and make life fun*

One big difference between chartering a yacht and owning your own is that you are not stuck with someone else's cutlery, crockery, pots, pans and all the other gear that makes a boat a home. If you are a diehard racing man or woman who is content to live on energy bars washed down with bottled water and sleep on a sail bag, you may not wish to read much further. However, most of us like to make our boats rather more comfortable and cosy. Don't underestimate the value of this: whether you are on board for lengthy periods or just the occasional weekend, you will almost certainly spend far longer using the boat as a home than actually sailing her. There is absolutely no reason why life afloat should be cold and spartan.

## CREW MORALE

### What's the point of going sailing with a grumpy crew?

At best you will be denying yourself much of the enjoyment of yachting; at worst you will find yourself on your own. Look after them, feed them well and make life fun. This is not a book on management and leadership, but the following notes may give you some ideas for enhancing the domestic aspects of sailing.

## WASHING-UP

Some domestic chores can't be avoided, and all crew members should take their turn with the washing-up – including the skipper. Similarly, encourage everyone to do some cooking. A bit of competition usually raises the culinary standards quite quickly.

## CATERING AND COOKING

As I have already implied, there is no need to live off tinned food and sandwiches just because you are in a (relatively) small boat. When I was sailing RN yachts in the late 60s the fare was beer and 'composite rations', as issued to soldiers in the field or as emergency supplies in warships. It was nutritious and reasonably healthy (not the beer, maybe), but pretty horrible for more than a day or so at a time. We soon found that even with just a couple of gas rings (no oven, grill or fridge in those days) it was perfectly possible to produce good, fresh meals, and it was fun doing so. Inevitably this engendered some culinary competition, and the standard continued its upwards trend. We never got as far as haute cuisine, perhaps, but we ate well.

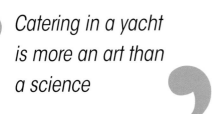

*Catering in a yacht is more an art than a science*

Now, many years later, we often run a family competition to see who can produce the best meal of a cruise. Marks are awarded for taste, presentation and, crucially, ease of washing- up. We have a rule that the cook does not wash up afterwards, so he or she is careful not to use an unnecessary number of pots and pans for fear of achieving low marks in that category.

There are many recipe books aimed at yachtsmen. Some of the best focus on 'one-pot' meals that can either be cooked on the hob or in the oven. These are great for producing hot, appetising food when sailing, without too much effort. Most can be prepared beforehand and simply heated up when required.

## Stowage

Catering in a yacht is more an art than a science, and stowage space for perishable foods is usually quite limited. However, if you use the bilges as a cool store for butter, bacon etc, and stow vegetables with plenty of ventilation – not stuffed into lockers – you may be surprised how much you can get on board. Stock up on what you need before the next shopping opportunity, plus a bit in reserve. Also keep a few 'emergency rations' in the form of vacuum-packed cooked meals, tins and other non-perishable foods. Soup, both tinned and in foil cartons, is invaluable as are packets of biscuits, pasta, jars of sauces, pickles etc. UHT milk may not be to everyone's taste but those little cartons are an excellent standby if fresh milk is not available or has gone off. One item we never sail without is a fruit cake or two. Ready sliced and wrapped in foil in an airtight container, it will keep for several weeks and can be eaten at any time of the day or night.

*The bilge is a good place for keeping drinks cool.*

## Cutlery and crockery

Fine bone china may not last long in a small boat, but you can get good sturdy plates, bowls and mugs that look good and will survive the usual knocks and bumps. Melamine and tough glass are both good choices.

# YOTTIE CAKE

This is a firm favourite for almost any occasion: with coffee or tea, in the morning or afternoon, during a night watch or whenever you need a tasty snack. It is also good as a pudding with cream, or as an accompaniment to a nightcap. It requires almost no culinary skill to make, and will keep for several weeks in an airtight container.

INGREDIENTS
450g dried mixed fruit
1 cup cold strong tea
1 egg, beaten
200g (1 cup) demerara sugar
240g (2 cups) self-raising flour

- Soak the fruit in the tea for several hours, preferably overnight.
- Add all the other ingredients and mix well.
- Put the mixture in a loaf tin and bake at gas mark 4/180°C for 1½ hours.
- Allow to cool. Eat!

NOTES
- Allowing the fruit to soak and absorb the liquid makes for a nice moist cake.
- Demerara sugar seems to work best, but any sugar will do.
- Substitute a slug of whisky, brandy or rum for some of the tea for added oomph.
- For a bit of variation, try including a few glacé cherries or dried dates in the mixture.
- Make plenty as it will soon go!

## Glasses

No drink tastes as good out of plastic as it does from a proper glass. Again, it is possible to buy quite tough glasses or you can press old Nutella jars into service. (There are probably other similar jars, but this particular spread is a favourite with one member of the family, so we have accumulated lots of them.)

There is no reason not to have a few wine glasses on board if carefully stowed. We keep ours in a locker fitted with 'drawer organisers', which keeps them nicely safe and secure.

*Drawer organisers keep wine glasses safe and secure.*

## Kettle and teapot

Check that both pour without dripping. It's easy enough to make a mess without the teapot doing it for you. A kettle with a whistle incorporated in a hinged lid over the spout is ideal. A separate whistle will wind up behind the stove or in the bilges before you can blink.

A metal teapot is best because it can sit on a recently used gas ring to keep warm.

*Choose your kettle and teapot carefully so they fit snugly on the stove-top and don't dribble when pouring.*

*Hot drinks do wonders for crew morale.*

## Pots and pans

If you are going to be doing a lot of cooking, don't skimp on quality. There is no need for top-of-the-range equipment but be wary of going for the cheapest possible just because it is going to be in the boat. Some chefs swear by stainless steel pans; I would go for non-stick any day. Here are some suggested items:

- Boaties® frying pan. Widely available in chandlers and perfectly designed for cooking in a boat. It is oblong and has a raised handle that fits over the stove-top fiddles. You can cook more sausages or bacon than in a round pan, and square fried eggs are a novelty.

- Two saucepans, one large one small.

- Small wok. Can double up as a saucepan or frying pan if necessary.

- Casserole dish. As large as the oven (if you have one) will take. Good for 'one-pot' meals. Choose one that can also be used on the hob.

## Non-slip mats

The ubiquitous knobbly rubber mats sold individually or in rolls are fine but can be difficult to clean. Look out for the smooth plastic variety (search for PVC mats on the internet); they are easy to clean and can be cut to fit any surface. They are particularly good on the galley work surfaces.

*A non-slip mat prevents spillages!*

## Water filter

Water stowed in the boat's tank may be perfectly safe but it does tend to adopt a flavour of its own. Some purifying products work well, but a filter really does make a difference. It can be fitted anywhere between tank and tap but the closer to the tap

# CUPBOARD LIGHT

Have you ever returned on board after a good run ashore and then scrabbled around trying to find the cabin light switch? How often have you searched for something from the back of a deep, dark locker? Or perhaps you just need to see the oil level on the gearbox dipstick. If so, the solution is a battery-powered cupboard light.

These are usually sold in packs of three from any decent DIY store, and come with self-adhesive fixings, so there is no need to drill holes in the woodwork. They are independent of the boat's electrical supply, and you turn them on/off by pressing the lamp itself – no fiddly switches.

We have one in the companionway, as shown, one in the engine compartment and one in the far end of the quarter berth (where there is no permanent light).

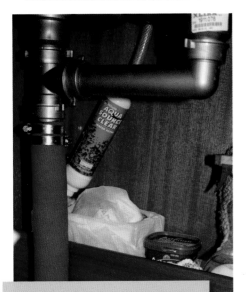

*A filter can greatly improve the taste of the water.*

the better. Filters come as cartridges – easy to renew – or in-line, which involves rather more plumbing to change.

## Fridge

Fridges in boats are a relatively new experience for me, but they are invaluable. Their one drawback is that they consume precious electrical power. Ask six yachtsmen how best to use the fridge while minimising power consumption and you will get six different answers. Most people are agreed that keeping it well stocked helps, as does keeping the lid closed as much as possible. Some have it on only when the engine is running or when

*Even just two rings and an oven can produce good food.*

*Secure bottles and jars to prevent breakages at sea.*

plugged in to shore power. Others keep the thermostat turned up high or have it as low as possible commensurate with doing the job of preserving food.

The best advice is to experiment with your own set-up and requirements. That said, if you get it really cold while plugged in, it should keep that way for at least 24 hours.

## OTHER DOMESTICS

### Shore power

Shore power enables you to charge the batteries without the need to run the engine. You can plug in or charge iPads, laptops and phones, and use electric kettles and toasters. Very few boats now don't have the facility to plug in to the mains. If not, it is a simple DIY job to install a basic system. The fittings are all readily available from chandlers or caravan shops, and only a rudimentary knowledge of electrics is required if all you want is a few 13A sockets. It is essential to incorporate a trip (RCD) in the system in case of shorts. If in any doubt, obtain expert advice.

A couple of cables connected together enable you to plug in to distant power sources without having miles of redundant flex when using an outlet nearer to the boat. When all the slots are taken, a splitter that allows more than one cable to use one socket is a valuable addition.

*A few 13A sockets make life alongside much more civilised.*

# SPLITTER

If you are rafted outboard of several boats, there may not be enough power sockets for everyone – and the first arrivals will have grabbed them before you! The answer is a splitter, which does exactly as it says: it splits the cable to provide two outlets from one inlet.

Commercial splitters are bulky and rigid, and you are unlikely to be able to fit more than one to the power pedestal on the pontoon. I have made up my own, which is more flexible and may be connected to your neighbour's power cable. The output arms (on the left) are then plugged into each boat – via an extension cable if necessary.

## Generator/solar panel

If you spend a lot of time at anchor or on a buoy you might consider investing in a small portable generator. There are many on the market and I tried several before going for a rather expensive model (coloured red, if that gives you a clue) that is very quiet and produces a maximum of 1000 watts. It just powers a small toaster and is ample for all other normal requirements, mainly battery charging. It uses little fuel and is so quiet that we can have it running in the cockpit without it deafening us. Being small and light, stowage is not a big issue. Well worth it.

We also have a small solar panel permanently fixed to the cabin top. It requires no attention but puts a trickle charge into the batteries most of the time during daylight hours. Portable and/or flexible panels are also available.

## Hot water

I am forever being nagged to connect up the built-in immersion heater. I have resisted so far on the grounds that hot water almost continuously on tap would just encourage the rest of the family to use water at a rate with which it would be hard to keep up. We have hot water after the engine has been running, and it doesn't matter how long your shore cables are, they are not much good at anchor or on a buoy. So they are not going to have hot water all the time anyhow; they may as well get used to it. That's my argument; you may think differently!

## Gas

There is not much to be said about gas except to be sure to have a spare bottle on board at all times. They only run out when cooking...

Instil in your crew the importance of turning off the gas supply every time they finish cooking. You should have a valve close to the stove, and it is this that should be used when the gas is not required for short periods. Turn it off at the bottle when leaving the boat, or overnight.

## Foul-weather gear/clothing

This is very much a personal choice, and you may not have had your own gear before. If so, be wary of buying vastly expensive offshore clothing if you will be sailing mainly in the summer in local waters with just the occasional longer passage. Breathable jackets and trousers are a must, and there is plenty of choice at the lower 'coastal' end of the market.

The same goes for footwear. Deck shoes increase in price according to the label and, while it would be folly to go for the very cheapest, don't be fooled into thinking that the more expensive ones necessarily provide better quality or durability. It is a good plan to keep one pair on board and another for shore-going. The grip on the soles is soon lost if they are regularly used for walking ashore. You will be aware of the range of yachting boots: many are excellent, but is it really worth spending hundreds of pounds if you are only going to wear them occasionally? When the going gets wet, short rubber wellies and thick socks are fine for me.

Always brief your crew to bring lots of warm clothes with them, and encourage them to wear at least one more layer than they think is necessary. It is much easier to strip off a layer when too warm than struggle to add more, usually under oilskins, when already too cold. Everyone should have a hat, however silly they may think they look. Even a baseball cap will help keep some body heat in.

## Bunks and bedding

There is no need to suffer hard plastic mattresses. Either invest in new ones or buy foam 'toppers' to make them more comfortable.

Many people still use sleeping bags – and they can be good temporarily or when space is at a premium – but if you are able to leave a bunk permanently made up, an under blanket, sheet, duvet and pillow is much more civilised.

## Stowage

We have touched on this before; it can be a real problem in some yachts, especially if you have a full crew. Despite my previous comments about warm clothing, warn

*A spare bunk can be pressed into service as a useful stowage space.*

crew members who may not have sailed much before that space is limited and to avoid bringing unnecessary personal gear – an oilskin jacket is fine for going ashore; no need to bring a separate coat. Allocate each member of the crew a space/locker for their stuff and discourage them from spreading it around the boat. Suitcases and boats are not made for each other. Encourage soft bags.

As for other, more permanent, gear – and it will grow over the years – a bit of imagination is needed. For example, is there a bunk that is never used? If so, take the cushion home and use the space for stowage. We have a small double after cabin that can only be used by two people who know each other very well. So the inboard, least accessible, bunk now houses the barbecue, toaster, generator, spare foresail and more. Use the bilges, the space under the bunks, cockpit lockers and anywhere else you can find. Just think what may be needed at short notice and what can be buried under other stuff. Every so often – perhaps once or twice a year – heave it all out, check it, note where it is, and put it back again.

## Entertainment

A built-in radio/CD/MP3 player greatly enhances the quality of life on board and is useful for local weather forecasts. You will need an LW receiver to get the shipping forecast on Radio 4; a small portable radio is ideal for this as it can be used anywhere. What else you have is, of course, up to you. Fixed televisions or computer screens have no place in our boat, but we do normally have a laptop with us for watching DVDs when stuck in harbour by the weather.

Cards and board games always go down well, although Monopoly has been banned with us. I can't think why.

## Heads

You probably have only one, and morale sinks very low, very quickly if there is a problem. Unless your powers of persuasion are considerably better than mine, the task of unblocking and maintaining the heads is firmly in your court. First, be strict in not allowing anything to be flushed that may cause a problem. Kitchen roll is a recipe for disaster, as are wet wipes and almost anything that hasn't already been eaten. Secondly, you don't need to understand how it works, just how to strip it down, fix it and put it back together – usually under pressure from the crew. Most heads are of a very similar design and spares are readily available. Keep a good stock on board, as halfway across the English Channel is not the best time to announce that the heads are out of order and won't be fixed until St Peter Port.

A common problem is weed or other debris blocking the inlet seacock. If you continue to pump in against resistance, you will only make matters worse. One solution is to remove the inlet pipe from the pump and blow through it using the dinghy pump. So long as the end of the pipe is above the waterline, no water will come inboard.

Actually, it is all remarkably simple but can be unpleasantly messy. Practice makes perfect. I know.

## First-aid kit

There is plenty of advice elsewhere (see *Reeds*) about first aid and what you should carry. It depends on your sailing area. For day sailing when help is close to hand, you just need to be able to patch up cuts and scratches and (hopefully) not much else. Mid-ocean is a very different matter and well beyond the scope of this book.

Wherever you are sailing, it is a good idea to enrol in a first-aid course; it could be a lifesaver, literally. Many are run specifically for sailors.

## Seasickness

Not many of us are totally immune to *mal de mer* but that is no reason to succumb to it. Much of it is in the mind and just the fear of seasickness can bring it on. Tablets and other remedies should be encouraged – always, of course, observing the correct dosage. A positive attitude, fresh air and keeping busy all help and can often stave off the onset completely.

If someone starts to look a bit green, put them on the helm or set them some other task. As skipper, you need to take extra care to ensure you remain capable of running the boat safely. I am very rarely seasick but, despite years at sea, you never get over it completely (ask Nelson), so I always take a tablet if in any doubt. It can do no harm, and you will soon discover what works best for you.

# SALOON

Someone once told me that every boat or ship should have a photograph of herself on display. I don't know why this should be, but I have done so in all my yachts.

One school of thought is that yachts should not be so luxurious that you are lulled into a false sense of security in what is, let's face it, a potentially hazardous environment. I go along with that to a degree – obviously you don't want so many soft furnishings that you can't get at the bilges – but some indulgences can turn a sparse cabin into a homely saloon.

A few pictures on the bulkheads, pleasant lighting and some scatter cushions make all the difference. A small ship's bell with a decorative rope also adds to the ambience. We don't use it to toll the hours, but it can be useful for waking slumbering crew.

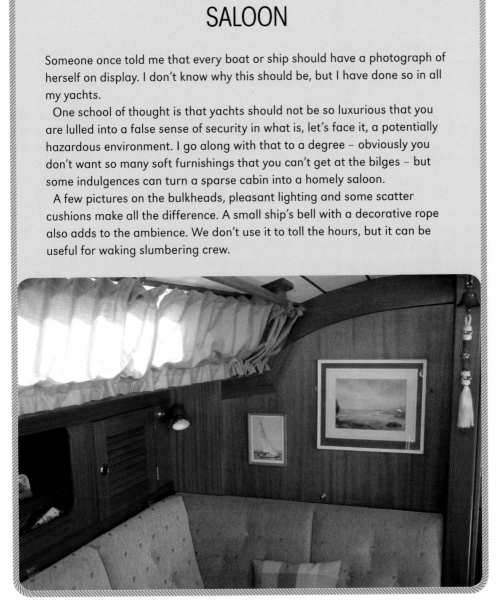

## Sunburn

Many inexperienced crew may not realise how damaging the sun can be at sea. Even on an overcast day, the effects can be far more pronounced than on land, and a liberal coating of sunscreen should be encouraged. On hot days, light, thin clothing that covers most of the body should be worn to prevent painful sunburn or sunstroke.

6

# ETIQUETTE

> *Most yachting etiquette has developed for good reason*

In this context, yachtsmen and women are all of one group and generally take a pride in conducting themselves courteously and considerately when in the company of other like-minded sailors – and, I am sure, at all other times. You don't have to abide by any particular code, but you will find that most yachting etiquette has developed for good reason, and non-compliance may make you stand out as someone who is unwilling or unable to 'do the right thing'. I am not for one moment suggesting that yachtsmen are an exclusive clique of people who have strange habits and rituals, but there are some customs that simply enable us to get the most out of our pastime and enjoy our time afloat to the full.

What follows, therefore, is by no means prescriptive. The examples I have chosen are some of the more obvious codes of conduct that you may wish to encourage your crew to follow. That said, times change and etiquette changes with them. What was frowned upon a few years ago may now be perfectly acceptable, and it is entirely up to you to decide how you and your crew conduct yourselves.

One note of caution: don't confuse etiquette with the law. The law requires us to wear an ensign when entering a foreign port, for example, but there is no law that says that you have to lower your flags at sunset or hoist them at a certain time in the morning. That is a matter of etiquette.

# FLAGS AND ENSIGNS

This old chestnut is probably more hotly debated than any other aspect of yachting etiquette: what flags should be flown, and where and when you should fly them. Let's look rather more closely at this potential minefield.

The 'order of precedence' for flying flags, other than the ensign, in a single-masted yacht is: masthead, starboard spreader, port spreader. So, if you are unable to use the masthead your next option is the starboard spreader. In this context, the masthead is 'superior' to the spreaders, which are, in turn, 'inferior' to the masthead.

## Ensigns

Ensigns, which by custom are 'worn' not 'flown', are national maritime flags and their use is largely dictated by law: the Merchant Shipping Act. The EU flag or regional flags are not ensigns and must never be worn as such. The ensign is only worn at the stern, usually on an ensign staff. Other rules apply for gaff-rigged or multi-masted vessels. The ensign is never worn at the masthead or from the spreaders.

Any British vessel may wear a red ensign, but a defaced red ensign (one that has a badge

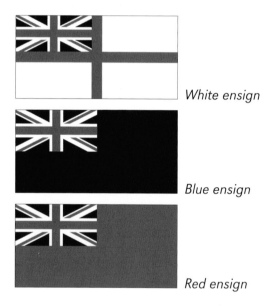

*White ensign*

*Blue ensign*

*Red ensign*

or symbol in the fly), and the blue and white ensigns, collectively known as special ensigns, may only be worn in accordance with a warrant issued by certain yacht clubs and associations on behalf of the Ministry of Defence. If you belong to one of these clubs, you may apply for a warrant that is unique to you and your yacht. In other words, it does not entitle you to wear a special ensign in someone else's yacht, nor may one be flown in your yacht if you are not on board or in effective control – ashore in the immediate vicinity, for example.

The warrant will spell out all the conditions of wearing the ensign. One of the most common is that you are obliged, again by law, to fly the burgee of the club or association that issued the warrant. If you want to fly the burgee of another club of which you are a member, you have the option of flying it inferior to the relevant burgee, or with a red ensign – with which you may fly any burgee or none at all. The white ensign is the exclusive preserve of the Royal Yacht Squadron and ships and establishments of the Royal Navy.

By law, an ensign must be worn when entering a foreign port.

## Burgees

A burgee denotes membership of a yacht/sailing club or association. It is usually triangular and may be of any design that cannot be confused with another club's burgee. It is traditionally flown at the masthead – some yacht clubs still insist on this – but modern rigs often make this impracticable, so it may be flown in an inferior position.

Some traditionalists maintain that you should fly only one burgee at a time – usually the 'senior' club of which you are a member. However, if you are sailing under the auspices of another club (of which you are also a member) and wish to fly that club's burgee, there is nothing to stop you from doing so. It is not uncommon to see yachts flying several burgees at the same time, but the order of precedence is important. If you are wearing a special ensign, the burgee of the relevant club must be flown superior to any other burgee. On the other hand, if you are wearing a red ensign – or no ensign at all – you are free to fly your burgees in any order you like.

## Other flags

Ensigns and burgees are not the only flags to be seen afloat. You may wish to show your support of, for example, the RNLI or RYA by flying their flags, and why not? This is where etiquette kicks in. Some people frown on strings of flags from every available position, others have no such qualms. It is up to you. I belong to an owners' association that is not a recognised yacht or sailing club but has its own flag. I often fly it at the port spreader in addition to any burgees. Personally, I think that a maximum of one flag in each position is about right. Many more and it may seem that you can't make up your mind or that you are showing off.

## Courtesy flag

This is a flag that deserves particular mention. It is a small version of a country's maritime ensign. Foreign yachts visiting the UK should therefore fly a small red ensign, not the Union Flag, as a courtesy flag.

Although not compulsory, you are expected to wear a courtesy flag when you are within the territorial waters (normally 12 miles offshore) of another country. Not doing so is bad manners and may justifiably cause grave offence. A courtesy flag is never flown at the masthead, nor should it be hoisted inferior to any other flags.

*A courtesy flag should be flown on its own on the starboard spreader.*

Indeed, with a couple of exceptions (see below), it should not be flown in the same hoist as any other flags. In practice, this means that it should be flown on its own at the starboard spreader. If necessary, transfer any burgees to the port spreader.

Sometimes you may wish to fly a regional flag as well as a courtesy flag – the Brittany or Normandy flags, for example. In this case it is perfectly acceptable to fly it below the courtesy flag in the same hoist. In the Channel Islands, where no courtesy flag is necessary, the relevant local flag may be flown instead.

## Q flag

The yellow Q flag indicates that your vessel is healthy and 'requires free pratique'. In other words, you are asking for clearance to enter harbour and go ashore. It should be flown when entering any non-EU country, but is not required when visiting the Channel Islands (which are not members of the EU) if arriving from the UK or France.

There are no firm rules about where to fly the Q flag. If your burgee is at the masthead, fly the courtesy flag at the starboard spreader and the Q flag to port. Otherwise, it is acceptable to fly the Q flag below the courtesy flag. As soon as you have cleared customs/immigration formalities, the Q flag should be struck.

*Dress overall whenever you feel like it!*

## Dressing lines

There are many reasons to dress overall – national celebrations, birthdays or any other occasion when you wish to show a bit of *joie de vivre*! There are no rules about how to dress overall but it is important not to cause any offence by inadvertently misspelling words or phrases. To get round this, there is guidance in *Reeds* and from the RYA on a suggested order of flags that will also provide a colourful display. Complete sets of signalling flags may be found in any chandlery. Two sets will contain all you need to make up your dressing lines.

Unless you intend to use your flags for signalling, keep your lines in separate bags – forward and aft – ready for hoisting whenever you feel the need.

## BERTHING ALONGSIDE OTHER YACHTS

It is customary to ask permission to go alongside another yacht as you approach. This even applies if you have been told to berth on her by the harbourmaster. Before you arrive alongside, make sure you have sufficient clean fenders rigged and ropes ready to be passed across. It is usually appreciated by the other boat if you have bights (spliced loops or a bowline) in the ends so that the ropes may be easily dropped over a cleat. Try to avoid chucking a mass of rope, expecting the unfortunate recipient to sort out the mess. Indeed, it is rarely necessary to chuck anything at all – wait until you are close enough to pass the ropes across.

Don't be afraid of asking the other yacht to secure your ropes in particular places. You may, for example, want a spring initially secured to a midships cleat to prevent the tidal stream from setting you astern before all the other ropes are made fast. Beware of the overenthusiastic helper whose one idea is to take a turn on the nearest cleat and hang on as though his life depends on it. If you are making headway, the chances are that you will then be 'sprung' heavily onto the other yacht. A polite but firm 'keep it slack, please' will normally be sufficient.

## Shore lines

Always be prepared to rig shore lines. It is unreasonable to expect the inboard yacht's cleats to take the weight of two or more boats in the same raft. Having rigged the shore lines, make sure they are tight enough to do their fair share. Once rigged, your bow and stern ropes to the other boat should be slack.

## Fenders

While it is common sense to rig fenders when going alongside, it is not necessary to rig them on your outboard side in anticipation of someone berthing on you. This can actually cause problems as both sets of fenders may become entangled as the other boat moves fore and aft. Let the outboard boat be responsible for her own fendering. If you don't think sufficient fenders have been deployed, by all means slip in one or two of yours when all the ropes have been secured.

You often see fenders secured to the top guard wire with just a clove hitch. This is fine for coming alongside, but a better arrangement in the longer term is to use a clove hitch on the bottom wire and an additional round turn and two half hitches on the top – much more secure.

## Crossing the raft

Again, it is courteous to seek permission before crossing another boat for the first time. When you cross, always do so forward of the mast, never through the cockpit. Cross as quietly as possible, especially when returning on board at night, and be sure your footwear is clean. Beware of open hatches, which can cause nasty and embarrassing accidents.

*Beware of open hatches*

*Make sure your fenders are well secured.*

*Always rig shore lines when berthed outboard of other yachts.*

## PONTOONS

Unless you are berthed on a finger pontoon by yourself, it is likely that other boats will need to share cleats with you. You therefore need to keep the cleats as clear as possible, allowing plenty of room for additional ropes. Don't secure your lines with lots of figures of eight; use a bight (loop) instead.

*This cleat leaves no room for any more ropes.*

Avoid the temptation of securing your lines by simply passing them round a cleat and back on board. Not only does this make it difficult for others to secure their ropes, but the risk of chafe is also greatly increased.

If you are single-handed, have all ropes prepared before you arrive and be ready to lasso a cleat as you come alongside. Whatever you do, don't leap ashore before at least one line is secured. If you do, and the wind is blowing you off, be ready to wave goodbye to your pride and joy!

## APPEARANCE

Most yachtsmen and women take a pride in how their boats are turned out. The greatest sin is to leave a fender over the side when underway. Always get them inboard as soon as possible after leaving from alongside. Other points to bear in mind when alongside, on a buoy or at anchor, are:

### Ropes

Coil them down or make a neat 'cheese' of the loose ends. Secure them to a guard wire to keep them clear of the decks. Coil and hang the mainsheet from the end of the boom. Don't leave spare ropes loafing around the deck; put them away in a cockpit locker or elsewhere.

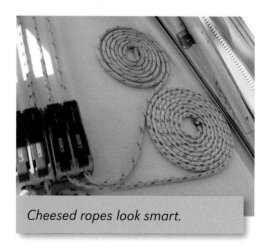

*Cheesed ropes look smart.*

*Always frap your halyards to prevent noise.*

## Halyards

Keep them taut and prevent them from frapping on the mast by using short lines to the shrouds. The main halyard may be secured to the end of the boom; genoa/spinnaker halyards may be led forward to the pulpit.

# DIPPING ROPES

Some mooring lines come with spliced bights (the black one above) or you may have to tie a bow line (blue rope). Either way, the trick is to 'dip' your rope by passing its bight through any others before putting it over the cleat.

This can be done with any number of ropes and, if they are all secured in this way, they can simply be released in any order without disturbing the others. Not many people seem to know this, but it makes life so much easier when the time comes to leave.

## Genoa sheets

These can get in the way of people crossing your boat. Consider running them round a suitable cleat or windlass on the foredeck then neatly along the decks to the winches. Don't just leave them flapping in the wind.

## Sails

Bag up hanked-on foresails or lash them neatly to a guardrail. Don't leave them in an untidy heap on the foredeck. Put the cover on the mainsail unless you are only stopped for a short time.

## Dinghy

Don't leave it on the outboard side to discourage others from coming alongside. At best it is unfriendly, at worst it will get damaged when someone berths on you regardless. If there is no room for it astern, it can normally be tucked in securely under the bows or on the pontoon.

There is nothing wrong with drying towels on the guardrails.

## Laundry

Some people scorn at washing hung out to dry. I see nothing wrong with this – within reason. Towels on the guardrails are, I believe, perfectly acceptable; some other items may need rather more discretion depending on the sensitivities of the people around you. Do I need to say more?

## Decks

It is a good idea to keep the decks clear of unnecessary clutter. Not only does it look messy, but you have an obvious obligation to keep your boat free of avoidable trip hazards. If crews of outboard boats will be crossing, have a look for potential dangers and irritations. I have already mentioned genoa sheets. Shore power cables are another example.

# UNDERWAY

## Waving

More a common courtesy than etiquette, it is usual for the helmsman (not necessarily the whole crew!) to raise an arm in greeting when you pass another yacht. It costs nothing and is a friendly gesture. If close enough, try to make eye contact. I find it very disconcerting when the other helmsman just stares fixedly ahead with no acknowledgement of my presence.

## Wash/wake

Sailing yachts do not make much wash, but be aware of others who might be affected: dinghies, canoes, swimmers etc. Either slow down or give them more room. Always go slowly in busy rivers or in amongst moorings.

*Always try to overtake to leeward.*

## Overtaking

Unless you are racing, try to overtake to leeward and thus avoid taking the other yacht's wind. If you can't get past this way, pass well upwind for the same reason. Similarly, in a near head-on situation when you are on the port tack and therefore the give-way vessel, consider altering your course to starboard rather than passing close upwind – but do it early enough to avoid any confusion.

## Dinghies

I see nothing wrong with towing a dinghy but there are some who consider it unseamanlike. Just be sure it is well secured. A couple of years ago, mine parted company without permission. To my embarrassment, it was returned to me by an RNLI inshore lifeboat, which had been alerted by a passing ship. They were very understanding, but I am now even more careful about securing it properly.

7

# ENGINE

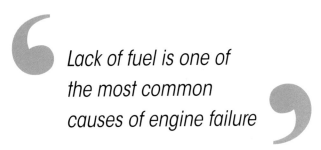

*Lack of fuel is one of the most common causes of engine failure*

Yachts' engines used to be known as auxiliary engines, implying that they were only used to get in and out of harbour if, and only if, sailing was impracticable. They were typically low-powered and slow. My first yacht's engine ran on petrol, was rated at 6hp, gave me about 4 knots and, if it started at all, could not be relied upon to keep running (particularly on the port tack for some reason). Modern diesel engines are dependable, relatively high-powered and will probably propel you almost as fast as you can sail, if not faster. Far from using them only when really necessary, we tend to motor whenever the intended ETA is looking unlikely or simply because we get bored. A pity, but that's life.

Whether we like it or not, a reliable engine is essential, and many harbour-masters insist that it is used in certain circumstances. So here are a few tips for preventing breakdowns. There is no substitute for the maintenance schedule laid down in the engine handbook, so you are strongly advised to follow it to the letter.

## Fuel

Lack of fuel is one of the most common causes of engine failure. Running out of fuel is inexcusable for any conscientious yachtsman, but fuel starvation can occur in even the best-maintained systems. This is usually the result of water in the fuel –

*A typical yacht engine. The jam jar on the left is for collecting overflow cooling water.*

difficult to detect as you top up – or the presence of 'bugs' that block the filters. The two go together as the bugs feed off the water, so the obvious solution is to reduce the risk of water contamination.

Try to get your fuel from reputable sources that have a high turnover of stock, and keep your tank(s) as full as possible to prevent condensation in the air gap between the fuel and the top of the tank. The easiest way of doing this is to top up from cans whenever you have used more than a few litres, or just visit the fuel berth more often. The inconvenience of doing so will be offset by your confidence in knowing that you are doing your best to minimise potential problems.

You may like to add additives to the fuel, which help disperse water and thus prevent the growth of bugs. There are several on the market, and they do seem to work, but I would still advise you to check the fuel occasionally.

Some tanks have a drain plug that can be opened (carefully!) to drain off water and any bugs that are living in it. If yours doesn't have one, or if it is inaccessible, try sucking out some fuel from the bottom of the tank using an oil sump pump into a clean container to see whether any bugs or water are present. If they are, keep sucking until the fuel is clear. A really badly contaminated tank may have to be completely drained and cleaned. This is a job best left to a specialist.

If you have a primary fuel filter with a water separator, you should be able to spot any water by shining a torch through the glass bowl, where any water will gather in the bottom.

As for running out of fuel, never take risks by delaying topping up until you reach a cheap source (eg, the Channel Islands). The few pounds saved are not worth it. Most yachts carry more than enough for normal use. In mine, which is a typical production boat, we have enough fuel for about 220 miles at 5.5 knots, or 40 hours under power with some in reserve. We very rarely drop below about ⅔ full.

## Oil

Check the oil at the start of every day. A sound engine will not use oil, so if the level drops you have a problem. Cloudy oil may indicate water contamination and this must be investigated as soon as possible.

## Water

Engines have either direct salt water cooling or indirect fresh water cooling. In the former, sea water is circulated around the engine, absorbs the heat and is ejected through the exhaust or, in some cases, through a separate outlet. A fresh water cooled engine is more like a car engine in that fresh water (with anti-corrosion additives/antifreeze) cools the engine and the heat is then transferred to salt water, which flows through a heat exchanger before being discharged overboard. In these systems, there are two pumps. The one for the fresh water needs little, if any, routine maintenance; the salt water pump – in either system – has a rubber impeller, which does need checking occasionally.

There are three things to keep an eye on: the water level in the heat exchanger/expansion tank for fresh water cooled engines; any debris in the salt water filter, if fitted; and a good flow of cooling water discharge. The most common causes of cooling water problems are either a blocked inlet or impeller failure. The latter often follows the former as the impeller tends to break up when the pump runs dry.

There is not much you can do about an underwater blockage – often caused by a plastic bag – except to try and remove it with a long-handled broom or by diving down. Sometimes, a blow through the inlet pipe using a dinghy pump can do the trick. You must, of course, be sure that the cooling water seacock is open. If you close it when leaving the boat, hang a label on the engine controls to remind you to open it before starting the engine.

As for the impeller, always carry at least one spare and make sure you know how to replace it. It is a simple but rather fiddly job that should only take a few minutes. You may have to shut the inlet valve to prevent flooding. Only replace it

*Salt water pump – the green arrow indicates the direction of rotation of the impeller.*

if you are sure that the inlet pipework is clear. If it isn't, you will be wasting your time. Also, coat the new impeller liberally with washing-up liquid (or whatever the manufacturer recommends) so that it is well lubricated before the water starts flowing again. If the old impeller has bits missing, they may have found their way into the heat exchanger, so have a look before it becomes a problem.

## Exhaust

We have mentioned water in the exhaust. The exhaust gases can also indicate the health of the engine; they should be almost colourless. Black gases may be caused by a lack of air (possibly a blocked air filter) or may suggest that more fuel is being delivered than required by the engine at a particular speed. For example, a wide open throttle but lower than expected revs may be the result of a rope or weed round the propeller, thus black smoke.

White 'smoke' is probably steam or just condensation. Steam may be caused by a blocked water intake; condensation will disappear when the engine warms up or the ambient humidity falls.

## Leaks

Keep the engine and engine compartment nice and clean. Always mop up any leaks or spillages so that new ones are readily apparent. A small dribble of water or oil may be able to be fixed quickly and cheaply. Ignore it and you could be letting yourself in for a breakdown (the engine, not you!) or an expensive repair. As you conduct your routine checks, have a good look around with a torch for any signs that all is not well.

## Batteries

Even a diesel engine needs more than air, fuel and water to keep it running sweetly. You may have one battery dedicated for starting the engine or you may have a switch that allows you to use any one. The advantage of a dedicated battery is that it should be designed to produce a short burst of high power, whereas domestic batteries are designed to produce lower power over a long period. The latter are also capable of a much deeper discharge cycle than those made for engine starting.

Whatever the layout, it is a good idea to be able to use any battery to start the engine. More than once I have been faced with a dead battery that appeared to be perfectly serviceable the previous day, so I have fitted an additional switch that enables me to cross-connect the domestic batteries to start the engine. For years I carried jump leads for the same purpose, but common sense eventually kicked in and I realised that getting at the batteries, identifying the correct terminals and connecting everything together in the right order – potentially at night in a rough sea while trying to enter a strange harbour – was simply not going to work.

Never open the main battery isolator switch while the engine is running. If you do, there is a good chance of writing off the alternator. A rotary switch (Battery 1–Battery 2–both) should prevent this. If you have separate switches, just be very careful.

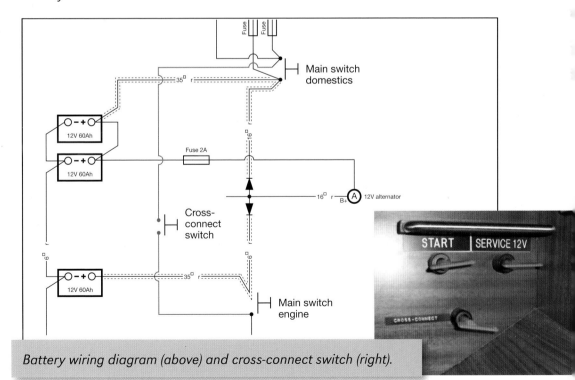

*Battery wiring diagram (above) and cross-connect switch (right).*

Batteries need to be charged. If you use your engine a lot, you may get away without a battery charger, but I doubt it. Modern luxuries such as heaters and fridges mean that electrical power is at a premium, and the engine's alternator won't keep up. Shore power, or a generator, connected to a charger will keep the batteries well charged. A solar panel is also worth considering; it will provide a trickle charge even on gloomy days. I am not a fan of wind generators – noisy and unsightly – but they have their uses.

## Spares

I cannot possibly list all the engine spare parts you need to carry; they will depend on your particular engine. Here are some that are common to most engines.

- Salt water impeller complete with a replacement gasket
- Oil filter
- Primary fuel filter and sealing rings – usually part of the water trap
- Secondary fuel filter and sealing rings – for the engine itself
- Engine oil – enough for a complete oil change
- Gearbox/sail-drive oil – may be the same as the engine oil, but not always
- Antifreeze – for fresh water cooled engines
- Alternator belt
- Selection of hose clips

## Toolbox

As with engine spares, it is impossible to provide a complete list of all the tools you need for routine maintenance, both for the engine and for all the other odd jobs around the boat. As a minimum you should carry:

- Spanners – assorted sizes, including at least one adjustable
- Mole grips
- Screwdrivers – straight and Phillips/ Pozidriv, various sizes
- Allen keys
- Pliers
- Wire cutters
- Small hacksaw
- Various washers, screws, nuts and bolts
- Cable ties

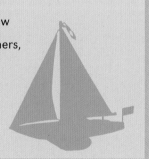

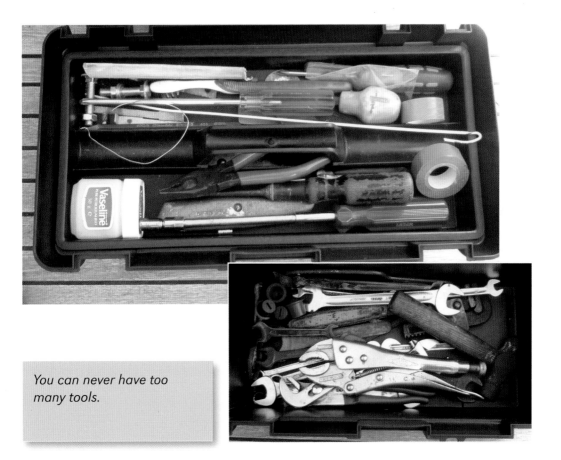

You can never have too many tools.

A final word on looking after your engine: diesels don't like running slowly or without load. Not only might they develop glazing in the cylinders, you will also risk a build-up of carbon in the exhaust system. This often happens in the elbow where the exhaust gases and cooling water meet. In extreme cases, so much carbon can be deposited that black smoke billows out of the transom even at low revs. As I can confirm, new exhaust elbows are expensive.

The solution is to run the engine hard. Some engineers advise giving it a full power run – throttle as wide open as it will go – for about five minutes every month or so. Try to avoid slow speeds for long periods, and never leave the engine idling while alongside for more than a few minutes. Get underway soon after starting it and shut it down as soon as you get back alongside. Under normal circumstances a good guide is to cruise at about 70% of maximum revs.

Even if you are reasonably clued-up about diesel engines, it is well worth enrolling on a course aimed specifically at marine engines. Courses endorsed by the RYA are recommended.

# UPPER DECK

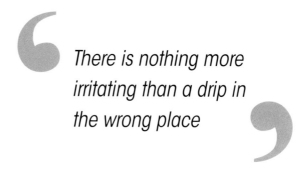

*There is nothing more irritating than a drip in the wrong place*

Until you became an owner, all the yacht's upper deck gear was provided for you. With your own boat you have the opportunity – indeed, the responsibility – to get everything as you want it and to your specifications. Your newly acquired boat will probably come with most of the essentials, but you might like to consider some of these suggestions now or when the time comes to replace various items.

## Anchors

There are many types and sizes of anchor on the market and, unless what comes with your yacht is hopelessly inadequate for your purposes, you will probably want to stick with what you have for the time being. That said, I bought one boat that had been sailed by her previous owners on the west coast of Scotland and came with a huge main anchor and about 60 metres of chain cable. I could hardly lift the anchor, and the cable was far more than I needed for cruising the English Channel. So I changed the anchor for a smaller version and landed 20 metres of cable. She also came, not surprisingly, with an electric windlass, which I kept.

The type/make of anchor will depend on where you are going to use it. Some are particularly suited to muddy bottoms, others hold well in sand and shingle. Personally, I still favour the CQR (or plough) as a good all-round anchor. Whatever

*Keep the upper deck clear of unnecessary clutter.*

you have, or choose to buy, you will regret skimping on size or weight. Do some homework and go for one that is appropriate for your boat in your sailing area – but be sure you can lift it!

### Kedge

A relatively small second (kedge) anchor can be invaluable, and is an essential spare should you have to slip your main anchor. Use it for short stays in calm conditions or in conjunction with the main anchor for additional holding power, to reduce your swinging circle or as a stern anchor in a narrow river or channel. A light anchor can also be taken off in the dinghy to haul the yacht off the mud when the navigation has gone awry – as it does with the best of us at times.

Beware of stowing a kedge anchor in a cockpit locker where it will become buried under ropes, buckets, dinghies and all the other stuff that tends to gather there. Ideally lash it to the pushpit where it can be rapidly deployed. Some people only use rope for the kedge but I prefer a few metres of chain with rope for the rest. If you are short-handed and use it for short-stay anchorages, run the rope outside the guardrails to the bow cleat, then drop the anchor from the cockpit, being careful that you don't drift over the rope and foul the propeller or keel.

A Danforth-type anchor is a good choice as a kedge as it stows flat and has reasonable holding powers.

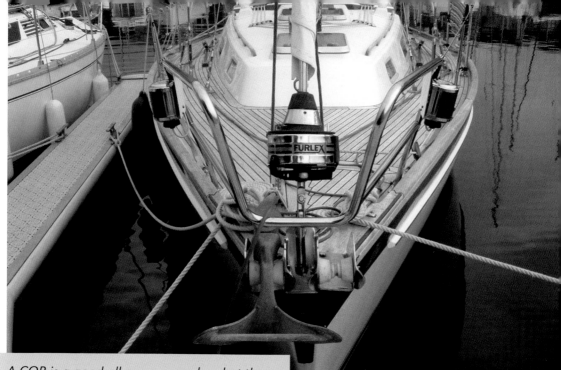

*A CQR is a good all-purpose anchor, but there are many other types to choose from.*

*Kedge anchor on pushpit. Keep the kedge anchor ready for use.*

# SAIL COVER

Lazyjacks have revolutionised the design of sail covers. Some traditional covers have slots to accommodate the lazyjack lines; others (like the one shown here) are permanently rigged on the boom and the lines are secured to the cover itself.

The advantage of this latter design is that there is no need to remove it before hoisting the sail – it simply unzips. The only removable item is the 'boot' that covers the forward end of the sail and secures around the mast.

If you are buying a sail cover for the first time, make sure that it is amply big enough for the sail to stow easily without having to struggle with the zip. Also, ask for battens on either side of the zip to allow the lazyjack lines to pass through the cover and the battens. This system is much more robust.

You will need slots for the reefing lines where they pass round the boom. Measure the positions of these carefully to avoid rips when tension is applied.

The obvious disadvantage of a permanently rigged cover is that it disturbs the airflow over the very bottom of the sail – not of great concern to the cruising yachtsman – but it does catch the sail neatly when reefing.

# FILLER SPANNER

Although the caps for the water and fuel filler pipes are usually designed to take a winch handle, space is often restricted. An old handle cut to fit solves the problem.

Always make sure the O-ring on the cap is in sound condition or salt water will find its way in.

Be very careful to check which filler you are using. I am not sure which is worse: fuel in the fresh water or water in the fuel. The latter may not be a disaster if you do something about it before starting the engine, but I doubt you would ever get rid of the taste of diesel in the fresh water tank.

## Cable markings

Whether you use chain or rope, you need to know how much anchor cable you have deployed. Too much is a waste of time and effort; too little and you will not stay put for long. For chain cable most yachtsmen agree that three times the depth of water is the absolute minimum on good holding ground. Rope requires at least five times the depth – and that's for the maximum depth you expect for the duration of your stay. If you are anchoring for an hour or so for lunch in a flat sea and little wind, you may get away with less, but keep your eyes open (literally!) for any signs of dragging.

You can buy coloured bits of plastic that fit between the links of chain, or you can use cable ties, available from any DIY store or electrician. Cable ties are easy to fit and provide very obvious marking – by sight or feel – but can be uncomfortable to handle. Coloured ribbon may be an alternative. At what intervals and with what colours you mark your own cable is up to you, but I suggest every 5m for the first 20m then every 10m thereafter.

I use red electrical tape wrapped round adjacent links: one link for 5m, two at 10m, three at 15m and four at 20m. After that I wrap the tape at wider intervals: a three-link interval for 30m, a four-link interval for 40m and so on. I also have a few links covered with a different colour tape that appears over the bow roller when the top of the shank is just emerging from the water. I can then have a look to see whether it is clear to start making way before getting it fully inboard and securing it for sea. Perhaps surprisingly, the tape stands up well to normal wear and tear, is kind on the hands and only needs replacing – cheaply and easily – about every other year.

## Other ropes and warps

I tend to hoard old ropes – my garage is full of them – as they will always come in handy at some time, and I fully confess to carrying far too many ropes on board. What you need is another matter. As an absolute minimum you should have four mooring warps, two shore lines and a rope suitable for towing.

### ■ Mooring warps

Avoid the ones with a spliced eye in one or both ends. The eye (bight) gets snagged on cleats and, if only on one end, it will be on the wrong end when you want it. It may also be difficult to pass through small fairleads or blocks. It is far better to make up a bowline whenever required. (A bowline, incidentally, is probably one of the most useful and common of all knots, and you and your crew should be able to tie one without thinking about it, in seconds and in the dark.)

Have all four warps the same length so any one can be used as a bow rope, stern rope or spring. They shouldn't be too long. If they are long enough to reach from your bow cleat to an inboard boat's bow cleat and back, that is about right. In my 34ft yacht the warps are 8 metres each and meet most situations.

### ■ Shore lines

One forward and one aft, and long enough to reach a pontoon or jetty from outboard of at least three other boats. When you rig them (always, unless the inboard skippers are happy for you not to do so) be sure that they are doing their work. If the shore lines are correctly tensioned, your bow and stern warps to the next boat inboard should remain slack.

### ■ Tow rope

As a minimum, this needs to be about 50 metres of three-stranded rope and large enough to tow another boat of a similar size. It is perfectly feasible to use two shorter ropes joined together (the shore lines, perhaps). A tow rope needs to have some elasticity, so plaited or pre-stretched rope is not suitable.

*Keep a long rope for towing – just in case.*

# SNUBBERS

These devices, usually rubber, prevent warps snatching and thus putting undue strain on cleats and other fittings.

There are many to choose from. Some have the rope threaded through and around them (top), whereas others can be rigged without having to undo the rope (centre). The latter can be fitted one, two, three or more at a time depending on the conditions. They can also be used on the mainsheet to dampen an unexpected gybe or on the mainsheet traveller to prevent snatching (bottom).

Warning: they don't float!

## Outboard engine

If you haven't got one already, choose the lightest engine that is capable of propelling the fully loaded dinghy. Speed in most rubber dinghies is not going to be more than a few knots anyway, so there is no point in having more power than necessary. You will usually have to lift the outboard over the side of the yacht, and this is made much more difficult if it is needlessly heavy. All new outboards now have to be 4-stroke – which adds to the weight – but you might find an older, lighter, second-hand 2-stroke.

Many outboard motors live buried in a cockpit locker, out of sight and out of mind. Unless yours is used regularly, don't depend on it starting at the first pull, or even at all. If it fails to start, it is usually just as the family are desperate to get ashore to the beach. Follow the maintenance schedule in the handbook and give it frequent runs.

## Dinghy

Having mentioned outboards, almost the opposite is true for dinghies: go for the largest that can be lifted on board and that can be conveniently stowed. Be wary of leaving it on deck the whole time. Not only does it get in the way, it is also vulnerable to theft and damage. A cockpit locker is ideal, but make sure you can get it out without too much of a struggle.

The fairly obvious reason for not skimping on size is safety. Large tubes and a good beam will make life more comfortable and less hazardous for the whole crew.

Dinghies are potentially dangerous, especially at night or with a strong tide running. With few exceptions – within a marina, perhaps – always insist on lifejackets being worn.

*Always wear lifejackets in the dinghy.*

*There is nothing wrong with towing a dinghy in calm conditions.*

# COCKPIT TABLE

A cockpit table is a real 'must' for any cruising yacht. If your boat has a wheel, a table may already be fitted on the forward side of the pedestal. If not, you have the choice of a free-standing 'picnic' table or one that attaches to the side of the cockpit. The latter provides flexibility as it can be swung to almost any position. In the picture you can just see the aluminium leg (on the left) that slides into a pad on the side of the cockpit locker. This has a hinged horizontal arm with another pad for the table top.

The fixings – securing pads, arm and leg – are usually supplied separately from the table itself. This can be bought, or you can make one to your own specifications.

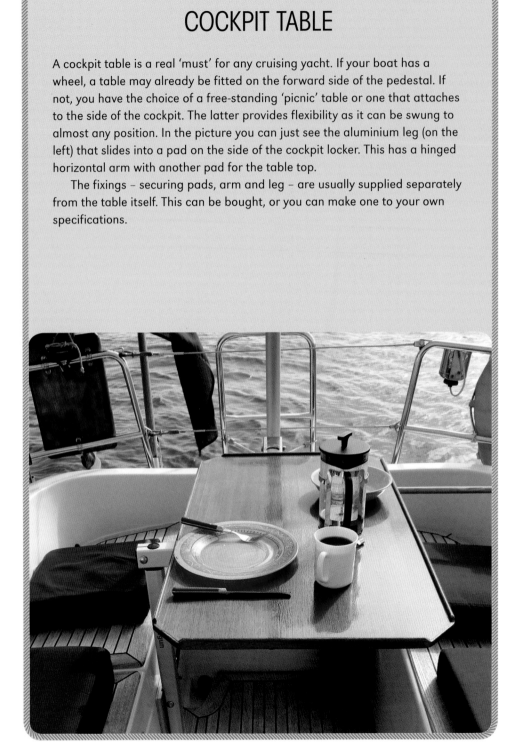

# BBQ

Food cooked al fresco is good; food cooked on a BBQ is even better.

Disposable BBQs, such as you find on garage forecourts, are great for the beach but not so practical in a boat, although you can get holders that keep them clear of the deck. A purpose-made, if rather expensive, BBQ is well worth adding to your inventory. The one shown above fastens to the pushpit, is well ventilated and has an adjustable grill and a lid. It takes about 20 minutes to get up to cooking temperature – like any other charcoal BBQ – and stays that way for at least an hour. So, when the sausages are done, there is plenty of time for the bananas baked in rum and brown sugar. Gas versions are also available, but the food is never quite the same without a bit of smoke!

Some marinas don't allow BBQs, so check before you light up. It is also a good idea to move the petrol can well away from stray sparks.

## Teak decks

They look great and help to insulate the boat from the scorching UK summer sun. The downside is that they can become unsightly with dirt and green mould. To keep them looking good, wash down frequently with plenty of water. Occasionally use a very mild acid solution to remove and deter mould, and encourage your crew to remove dirty shoes before stepping on board. Don't scrub teak decks vigorously and never use a power washer on them. Some owners apply teak treatment or stains, but they never seem to be an improvement over bare wood.

## Hatches

Inspect hatches frequently and test for leaks. They are all that keeps the water out – rain or sea – and there is nothing more irritating than a drip in the wrong place. They may also be an escape route in an emergency, so the fastenings must be easy to operate.

Hatch perspex will in time become crazed with exposure to the sun. On the whole this doesn't affect its integrity or strength, but it is not a pretty sight, particularly from the inside. The only solution is to renew the perspex, an expensive job best left to a professional. You can greatly extend its life by fitting canvas covers that at night keep out the light and prying eyes if you don't have hatch curtains.

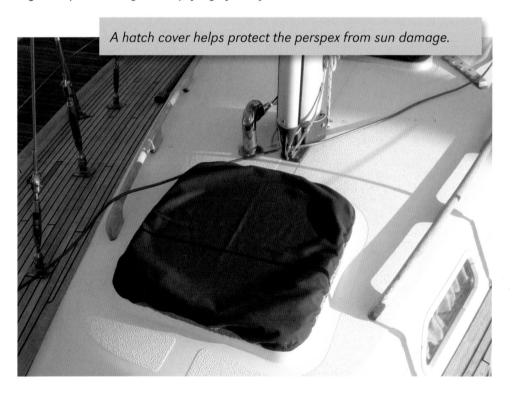

*A hatch cover helps protect the perspex from sun damage.*

# SECURE TILLER

If there is a tide running, or if the boat is moving around in the wind when at anchor or on a buoy, the tiller must be secured to prevent it sawing across the cockpit. Often this is achieved by lines taken to both sides of the cockpit coaming.

A neater and more secure arrangement is to adapt a length of dowelling (or broom handle) to slot into the autopilot fittings. Obviously this depends on you having a tiller pilot! If not, you are back to lines. Or you could adapt it some other way.

Beware of leaving the tiller raised and lashed to the backstay. In most cases this will not prevent it from swinging about. It is fine in still waters, but not much good in a tideway.

# RIGGING AND SAILS

*A cruising chute can be a real bonus in light airs*

## SAILS

Your sails are the most valuable items in the boat, not perhaps in financial terms but certainly as far as propulsion is concerned. Good sails that are well maintained will last for many years. If you ignore them, they will become grubby, develop defects (minor tears etc) and be subjected to salt crystals, which in turn will attack the stitching.

### Maintenance

Take every opportunity to give them a fresh water wash: sail in the rain occasionally or use a hose. Be sure to do this before packing up for the winter. You may like to take them for a professional wash/valet. If you do this through a sailmaker, you can also have the sails given a thorough check for signs of wear and tear, and have repairs done before they become critical.

### How many?

The number of sails you carry will depend to a great extent on your sailing activities. For the average cruising yacht with a roller reefing headsail, an absolute minimum will be a mainsail and a jib/genoa. However, a large genoa does not usually set well

*Trim the sails for best performance.*

when more than a few rolls are taken in, so an additional, smaller foresail is worth having for those trips when the forecast is for breezy weather. A working jib, which you can carry in winds up to, say, force 5 or 6 without reefing, will complement the genoa nicely, and the boat will sail far better.

## Spinnakers

I don't consider a spinnaker to be a cruising sail (many disagree with me) but a cruising chute can be a real bonus in light airs. To make life easy, either invest in a separate furling stay or have a snuffer, which pulls down over the sail while it is still hoisted.

## Storm sails

Storm sails are a matter of much debate. If your sailing consists mainly of cruising in home waters – UK and adjacent continent – and you are a reasonably prudent skipper, storm sails will probably never be necessary. A mainsail that can be reefed by at least 40% of its full size and a stout working jib will see you through the occasional hard blow. Regular offshore sailing in all weathers, on the other hand, calls for a trysail and storm jib. If this is your scene, don't wait to bend them on until conditions have deteriorated so much that it becomes difficult or even dangerous to do so.

## Reefing

If your mainsail is reefed by rolling into the mast or boom – a method that is becoming increasingly common – the size is infinitely variable all the way down to nothing. The only snags with this system are that the sail can become jammed, and it will provide very little power when deeply furled. The former is, at best, embarrassing; the latter could be distinctly hazardous if you are trying to claw off a lee shore. The advantage of this system is that reefing is quick and easy, and can be done from the safety of the cockpit.

*A cruising chute is useful for light winds.*

Joining an owners' association provides opportunities for rallies and other events.

*The time to reef is when you first think of it*

If you have slab reefing (separate lines for the tack and the clew) or single-line reefing (with blocks and ropes inside the boom), the procedure may be more convoluted but you will end up with a sail that sets better and therefore produces more power.

The area by which the sail can be reduced by single-line reefing depends on the length of the boom, and this may not be sufficient for all conditions. You should therefore rig additional lines for a deep reef. This may involve a trip to the mast to secure the tack, so take this reef in (as with all others) earlier rather than later. The line for the clew will be quite long and may spend most of its time flapping in the breeze, but don't be tempted to rig it only when needed. No one wants to be standing on the cockpit coaming struggling to reeve a line through a cringle in the leech in a force 7.

## Cunningham

It is often difficult to fully tension or adjust the luff of the mainsail by use of the halyard alone unless the boom is capable of moving up and down the mast on a short track. One solution is to have a cunningham. This consists of an eye a short way up the luff through which a line passes, usually controlled by a small tackle, to increase the tension. If your sail is not already fitted with this, get your sailmaker to put in the necessary cringle. You may be amazed at the difference it can make to sail shape and the power/speed it will produce.

## HALYARDS

These are often the weak link in the rig. They are subjected to lots of wear where they pass round sheaves, and the splices (or knots) for the shackles can fail. The topping lift may be a useful substitute for the main halyard, and the spinnaker halyard, if rigged, may just be pressed into service as a spare genoa halyard, although the lead will not be ideal. It is best to check regularly and renew them if in any doubt.

# CLUTCHES AND COAT HANGERS

Clutches, or jammers, are now widely used instead of traditional cleats for many ropes: halyards, reefing lines, topping lifts, kicking straps et al. They are simple to use, reliable and effective, but they do need to be marked so that anyone can see which clutch controls which rope. You can get pre-printed labels, but Dymo tape works just as well.

Threading ropes through the clutches can be difficult. If they go through easily, they are probably too small. This is where a wire coat hanger comes into its own. All you need is a small loop of whipping twine sewn onto the ends of all the relevant ropes. You then pass the wire, with a short hook, through the clutch, snag the loop and pull it back. Simple.

In fact a short length of stiff wire is one of the most useful items in your toolbox and can be used for a multitude of jobs – many of which you haven't yet thought of! A cut coat hanger always seems to be best – if you lose it, there are plenty more where that one came from.

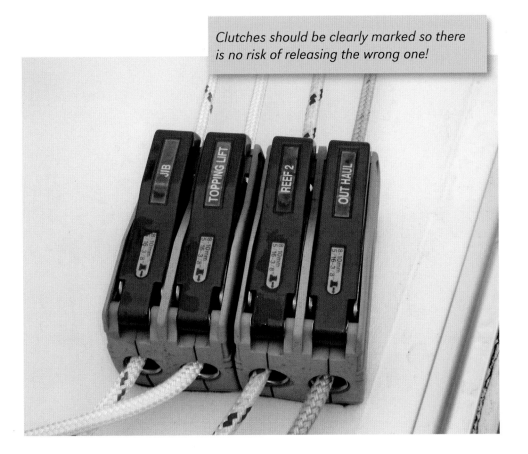

*Clutches should be clearly marked so there is no risk of releasing the wrong one!*

10

# REGULAR MAINTENANCE

> *Always check out a salt water leak without delay*

Routine maintenance is something you can't avoid. From your experience of sailing other people's yachts, you will be aware of the checks that need to be conducted on a regular basis. With your own boat there is one big difference: cost. I know how easy it is to ignore a potential problem in the hope that someone else will fix and pay for it later. In your own boat you will quickly find that keeping your eyes skinned for signs of wear and tear will save you large repair bills, not to mention the inconvenience of replacing or repairing an item that might otherwise have had years of useful life in it.

A sail torn on an unprotected split pin might involve an expensive visit to your sailmaker, whereas a piece of tape round the offending pin will cost almost nothing and will take just a few minutes. Lack of cooling water in the engine could spell disaster – not only for the engine but also, in confined spaces, navigationally – but a regular check on the exhaust will alert you to the problem before it becomes critical. An unusual amount of water in the bilges might indicate a leaking seacock, a fault with the fresh water system or merely overenthusiastic washing of the upper deck with a hatch left open.

Whatever the cause, if you spot something out of the ordinary, check it out. This comes under the heading of continuous monitoring. More extensive checks, perhaps to a written schedule, need to be carried out at specified intervals.

Some people choose to do all the maintenance themselves, others pay their marina, boatyard or another contractor to do it for them. However, as I have indicated, a responsible and prudent yacht owner must carry out routine preventative maintenance on a near-continuous basis. You can't expect someone else to check for normal wear and tear while you are out sailing, just as you would not expect your car passenger to react to a dashboard warning light. It's your problem, and you must decide what action needs to be taken.

## Photographs

Take lots! Photos of mast fittings are especially useful for briefing the person who is to be hoisted aloft about exactly what needs to be done and how the relevant item fits together. It is also a good idea to take a photo of almost anything before you take it apart. If ever you have to disconnect all the wires between the radar aerial and the display, you will see what I mean.

If you are buying new, try to take photos of wiring and pipework before it is concealed behind furniture and fittings.

What follows is by no means exhaustive as each yacht is different and you will have to decide where your priorities lie. Seasonal maintenance – which is usually done when the boat is out of the water – is covered in more detail in the next chapter.

# DAILY CHECKS

Most of these should be done before sailing, and can be completed in a few minutes while you prepare the boat. Others can be done while you are underway as part of your continuous monitoring routine. There is no need to climb the rigging or take the engine apart, just keep your eyes open.

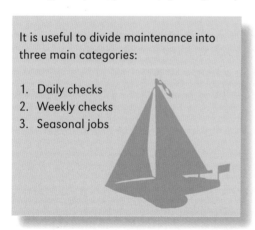

It is useful to divide maintenance into three main categories:

1. Daily checks
2. Weekly checks
3. Seasonal jobs

While you have nothing else to occupy you, get hold of the binoculars and have a look up the mast to see that all is well. Some years ago I was doing this while enjoying a bit of sunbathing and noted that the clevis pins holding the spreaders to the mast were all upside down! No real disaster, but I soon had someone up the mast putting things right – what else are light and nimble children for?

## Running rigging

Look for: chafe; shackle pins working loose; ropes coiled neatly and ready for use; halyards not twisted round other ropes (the main halyard and topping lift are frequent offenders); foresail or spinnaker halyards not fouling the rolling reefing gear near the top of the mast ('halyard wrap' can write off a forestay).

## Standing rigging

Split pins all present and opened out correctly; clevis pins secured; no broken strands near the terminals; stays/shrouds at correct tension. Look up the mainsail track while sailing to see that the mast is still straight. If it isn't, a rigging screw may be working loose.

## Deck gear

Nothing working loose; winches all free to turn; anchor secured; boathook available.

## Safety gear

Test the lifebuoy light to see whether its batteries are fully charged. If you have a telescopic dan buoy make sure it is fully extended. When deployed, the flag on the end should, of course, be as high as possible, and you really don't want to extend it as someone falls over the side – you and your crew will have many more important things to do.

*Halyards at the foot of the mast. In some boats they are led aft to the cockpit, which can make sail changing and reefing more convenient and safer.*

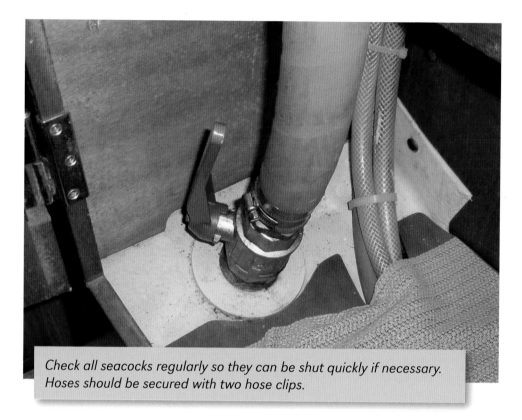

*Check all seacocks regularly so they can be shut quickly if necessary. Hoses should be secured with two hose clips.*

## Engine

Oil level; water level in the expansion tank (if fitted); gearbox oil; leaks (water or oil); unusual vibration or noise when running; water coming out of the exhaust; exhaust gases reasonably clear (black smoke may indicate blocked air intakes; steam is a sign of overheating).

## Seacocks

Check that easily accessible ones are free to turn; heads and galley seacocks off (if risk of flooding while sailing).

## Log impeller

Free to spin. If it is tricky to remove, check that the speed read-out looks about right when underway and is not under-reading significantly. A short burst astern on the engine may blow away the odd bit of seaweed, otherwise it will need to be raised and cleaned.

In some areas, and particularly in warm water, the impeller can get fouled up very quickly. Consider raising it when you leave the boat for more than a few days. A light smear of vaseline can help to deter marine life and stave off the growth of weed.

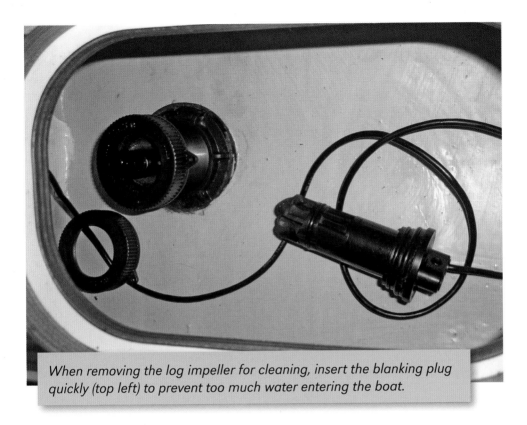

*When removing the log impeller for cleaning, insert the blanking plug quickly (top left) to prevent too much water entering the boat.*

## Bilges

These should be dry. If there is any water, is it fresh or salty? Fresh water is probably from a deck leak (see below) or from the fresh water system. It is more likely to be irritating rather than hazardous. Salt water is potentially more serious as it could indicate a weeping stern gland, faulty seacock, detached hose connection or something even more worrying such as loose keel bolts. Like oil or fuel in the bilges, always check out a salt water leak without delay.

## Leaving boat checks

While we are thinking of daily checks, I find a list of 'leaving boat checks' saves me from worrying about what I may have missed ('Did we turn the gas off?') or forgotten to take home. Many of these relate to the appearance and security of the boat, but some come firmly under the banner of preventative maintenance. Halyards secured away from the mast will prevent undue wear and chafe; well-secured fenders avoid expensive gel coat repairs; instrument covers prevent sun damage to the screens. My list, which I keep in the boat's data book, includes the following. You may think some of these are blindingly obvious, but it is so easy to overlook something when the pressure is on to get home. As usual, the list is not exhaustive.

| Below decks | |
|---|---|
| Fridge | Lid open – to prevent smells and mould |
| Main switch panel | All switches off |
| Batteries | Main switches off – to avoid battery drain |
| Engine | Seacocks closed; key removed |
| Windows & hatches | Closed and locked |
| Heads | Inlet/outlet valves off |
| Bilge | Pumped dry |
| Gas | Isolating switch closed |

| Upper deck | |
|---|---|
| Ensign and burgee(s) | Lowered |
| Instrument | Covers on |
| Sail cover | Secured |
| Backstay | Slackened (if you have a fractional rig) |
| Halyards | Secured away from mast |
| Tiller | Secured amidships – prevents wear on bearings |
| Cockpit lockers | Locked |
| Fenders | Correctly positioned and secured |
| Warps | All secure; snubbers fitted if necessary |
| Gas | Turned off at the bottle |
| Main hatch | Locked |

And you may like to add, as I do, a reminder to take home house keys, spectacles, mobile phone etc.

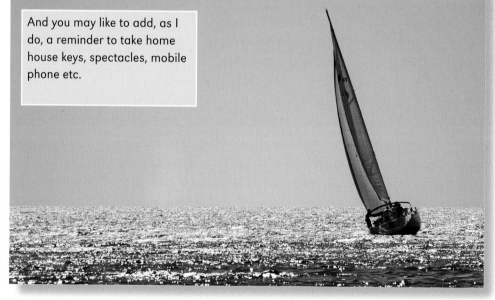

*Winches are often neglected but they do need servicing annually.*

## WEEKLY CHECKS

A bit of a misnomer, perhaps, but these are some of the checks that need doing on a regular basis, but perhaps not every time you go sailing, depending on how often the boat is used. In addition to your daily checks:

■ **Running rigging**
A closer look for areas of chafe – use binoculars for checking ropes where they pass round sheaves near the top of the mast; check that little-used ropes are free to run – spinnaker halyard and associated gear, perhaps.

■ **Standing rigging**
Use binoculars to look for potential problems; run your hands (be careful!) up and down the rigging as far as you can reach to check for bulges or split wires; if in any doubt, go up the mast for a closer look. Examine the terminals for cracks.

### ■ Deck fittings

A more detailed inspection than daily checks; give everything a good tug.

### ■ Engine

Be guided by the manufacturer's handbook; use a torch to check for any leaks; check security of all hoses; inspect the salt water weed trap, if fitted, for signs of weed and debris; look for any water in the primary fuel filter water trap.

### ■ Seacocks

Crawl around and check them all; work the handles/wheels to ensure they are free; check the hose clips for security (they should each have two hose clips).

### ■ Log impeller

Remove and clean it at intervals depending on how much fouling it is subjected to; a clean impeller will give more accurate readings – particularly important if it feeds speed information to your radar and other electronic devices.

### ■ Instruments and navaids

If they are used infrequently – radar, perhaps – turn them on and give them a good workout. This has the added advantage of keeping you familiar with their controls and features. The radar will not produce a good picture when in a crowded marina or other enclosed space. To check it thoroughly – and to gain experience – run it while underway in reasonably open water.

### ■ Lights

Turn on all navigation and deck lights, and check they are all working.

### ■ Deck leaks

These can be surprisingly difficult to track down. The first sign may be fresh water in the bilges but the source may be almost anywhere. Open all the lockers and other spaces under the side decks and check for dampness or drips. Guardrail stanchions and other fittings that are bolted through the deck are well-known culprits for working loose and allowing water in.

# SPARE PARTS

Beware of throwing anything away unless it is clearly beyond any useful purpose. When a shackle fails or, more likely, goes over the side, you need to have a spare, and know where it is. The same applies to a plethora of 'come in handy' gear. Here is a list to get you thinking. It is by no means comprehensive but will give you some idea of what you might need.

- Shackles – all shapes and sizes
- Split pins – old ones can be used again if not critical to safety
- Screws – various sizes and lengths, brass and stainless
- Electrical tape – can be used for much more than just wiring
- Masking tape – its uses are almost limitless, from leak stopping to oilskin repairs
- Blocks/pulleys
- Rope – you can't have too much
- Twine and small cordage
- Softwood bungs – for leak-stopping
- Plastic tubing – for replacing water pipes, syphoning fuel etc
- Light bulbs – cabin lamps, navigation lights, instrument lights etc
- Electrical cable – various lengths and sizes
- Cable ties
- Battery water
- Engine oil – and gearbox oil if different
- WD40 – for anything!
- Small oil can – with light oil for routine maintenance
- Fresh water – a few litres for emergency use if the main tank becomes contaminated
- Vaseline/petroleum jelly – multitude of uses
- Lifejacket gas bottles and automatic inflation devices (rearming packs)
- Batteries – AA, AAA etc, as required

Stowage might pose a problem, but so long as you know where everything is (make a list if necessary) any available space can be pressed into service. Most of my bits and pieces live in plastic boxes under bunks or in the bilges. If you really can't find room on board, keep surplus spare gear at home and replace it in the boat when necessary.

# SPLIT PIN

These little pieces of bent wire prevent your mast falling down! So, it is worth inspecting them regularly and renewing them if in any doubt.

A split pin does not have to be opened fully and wrapped round the clevis pin. Not only is this unnecessary but it also makes removal very difficult. Ends opened to about 30° is ample. In the picture below, the pin is OK but could perhaps be opened out just a bit more.

I like to be able to see my rigging and fittings at a glance. However, if the pins are likely to damage sails or legs, they must be covered with tape.

11

# WINTER MAINTENANCE

*The main thing is to keep the boat well ventilated*

Some maintenance work can only be done when the boat is out of the water, but this does not mean that she has to be ashore for the entire winter. Nevertheless, you will have to have her lifted, even for just a short period, to apply the antifouling each year, and this is the time to inspect all those parts that are normally under water.

Many owners tend to contract out these winter jobs, but if you do them yourself you will not only save money, you will also develop a better knowledge of your boat. Can you be sure, for example, that a boatyard will spot signs of osmosis before they apply another coat of antifouling? Will they note a gel coat scratch as they polish the topsides? Will your local engineer do a thorough job when he changes the engine oil? If you do it yourself you will know that all is well. That said, unless you are particularly competent, gel coat repairs, changing the seal on a sail-drive unit and renewing the rudder bearings are probably best left to the professionals.

## LAYING UP

Whether you lay up ashore or leave the boat afloat for the winter depends on available facilities and, possibly, the cost of lifting out, storage etc. There is much to be said for keeping the boat in commission all year, just coming out of the water

*You must use special antifouling on the sail-drive. Paint used on the hull is not suitable.*

*A simple, cheap but effective winter cradle may be made from scaffolding.*

for a few days to scrub off, antifoul and check that all is well below the waterline. Pick your days, and winter sailing can be a delight. However, let's assume that you are going to lay her up.

## Cradle/supports

If the boat is to be laid up ashore, no doubt your club, marina or boatyard will take a healthy interest in how she is supported. Wooden shores are fine, but a well-fitting cradle is probably the most secure arrangement for real peace of mind during stormy winter nights.

Purpose-built cradles can be horrendously expensive but scaffolding is an effective and cheap alternative. All you need are about 20–30 lengths of scaffolding tube, the appropriate swivel connectors and some adjustable bases for the shores themselves. Take your time to design the cradle (look at how other owners have done it) and build it round the boat while she is temporarily supported by other means. Make sketches and take lots of photographs for future reference.

If all the tubes are the same length, there is no need to mark them or use the same ones in the same places each time. All the bits are readily available from a builders' merchant and, with very little maintenance, will last for ever.

## Ventilation

Some owners take everything moveable out of the boat, others barely do anything. If you have a small heater or a dehumidifier (and access to electricity), you may like to leave most of the gear on board, but it is usually wise to remove expensive electronic kit, outboards and personal belongings. However, space ashore may be a problem. My

# WINTER COVER AND WINTER ASHORE

There is much to be said for laying up ashore. The hull gets a chance to dry out (not so critical for newer boats) and you have plenty of time to get on with the annual maintenance. Having said that, fin/long keel yachts with their masts stepped are vulnerable to stormy weather, and even bilge keels have been known to 'walk' across hard standings. However, a good cradle or shores should hold her and keep her safe.

Laying up afloat also has its attractions. The boat is probably safer from storm damage (lots of fenders and ropes), and there will be less strain on the rigging as the boat is free to roll with the blows. You will need to have her ashore for at least a few days to recoat with antifouling and do any other underwater jobs.

Covers are a mixed blessing. A well-fitted one that envelops the whole boat, like the one above, will keep everything clean and dry. But a tarpaulin casually lashed down may well work loose and may even cause damage if left to flog in the wind.

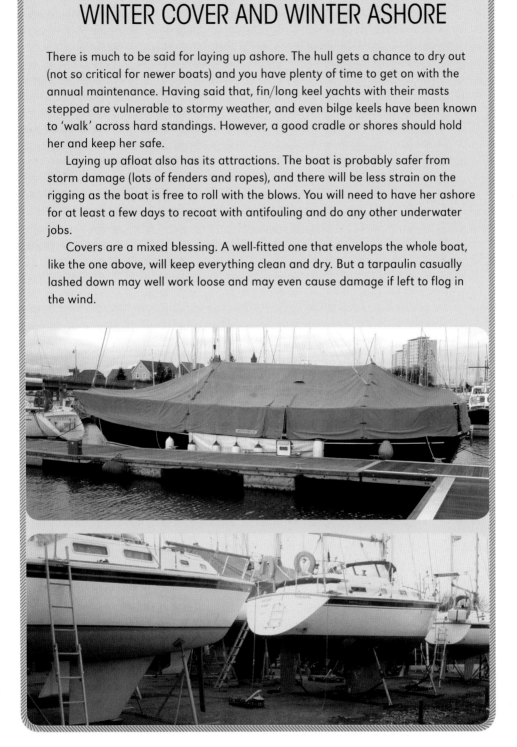

*Use a small electric heater to keep the frost at bay during the winter.*

lay-apart store at home (which my wife erroneously refers to as the spare bedroom) is just about big enough if I commandeer some loft space as well. However, there is little point in transferring gear from a damp boat to a damp shed or garage.

The main thing is to keep the boat well ventilated. Don't be tempted to seal her up as a good flow of fresh air will ward off damp and mildew. If she is ashore, and there is therefore little risk of her being stolen, you might remove a washboard and leave the hatches ajar. If you do this, remove any valuables from below. Keep the rain out with a well-placed tarpaulin or, best of all, an overall winter cover.

## Mast

Should you unstep the mast or leave it standing? The process of removing it may risk damage and be more trouble than it is worth. If remaining afloat, the mast is probably best left stepped. Ashore, if you have confidence in your cradle or chocks and there is no good reason to take it out, leave it alone. But in particularly exposed locations you will probably sleep better knowing that the extra windage of mast and rigging is not threatening the boat as the wind howls. Some people recommend easing the rigging screws by a turn or two to prevent distorting the hull.

The mast and fittings must be given a good check at least once a year, preferably before the sailing season gets underway. You may be happy to do this yourself or you may prefer to pay someone to do it for you. I would recommend that the mast should be unstepped at least every 3–4 years for a really good-going over.

*The mast will appreciate a wash down. Radar performance is improved if the radome is kept clean.*

# MAST SHED

If you unstep your mast for the winter, protect it well. A horizontal mast will collect copious amounts of dust and dirt, so wrap it in plastic sheeting or, better still, put it under cover. A nice dry mast shed is ideal and allows you to thoroughly inspect the mast in relative comfort.

Take the opportunity to examine all the fittings, especially where the standing rigging attaches to the mast. Check the sheeves (at top and bottom) for excessive play, and have a look at all the electrical cables for signs of chafe. Finally, give the whole thing a good wash with soapy water.

## Sails and running rigging

Whatever you decide to do with the mast, be sure to remove the sails, not only to reduce windage but also to give them a thorough check and/or clean. I usually remove the running rigging (halyards, topping lift etc) for the same reasons and to prevent chafe. Light lines rove in their place avoid the need to climb the mast to put them back again.

Bear in mind that most insurers expect you to undertake 'reasonable care and maintenance'. Unless you can show that the mast and rigging have been properly and regularly inspected, a claim for rigging failure may not succeed.

## Standing rigging

It is often assumed that the standing rigging in a cruising yacht (which is not used for racing) should be replaced every ten years. Few insurers insist on this, and a professional rigging check or electronic testing may well suffice to extend its useful life without invalidating your insurance cover. To spread the cost of renewing the rigging, I have adopted a rolling programme of replacement: the forestay one year, backstay the next, cap shrouds the next, and so on. After three or four years I then have at least another six years before starting again.

## Engine

You will find advice on winterising the engine in the relevant handbook. As a minimum, an oil change at the end of the season is usually recommended. Don't be tempted to leave this until the start of the next season. Old diesel oil is corrosive and should not be left in the sump over the winter. The antifreeze should be checked in fresh water-cooled engines; a good flush through is necessary for salt water systems. Remove the salt water impeller to prevent distortion or, better still, treat the engine to a new one at the start of the year.

Of course, if you use the boat during the winter, there is no need to winterise, just change oil, filters etc as required by the routine maintenance schedule.

## Batteries

Ideally, take them ashore and give them a charge every so often to keep them in peak condition. However, they are heavy and probably difficult to get at, so either charge them *in situ* or have a solar panel or wind generator do it for you.

## Seacocks

Take the opportunity of the boat being out of the water to remove the pipework (which should always be secured with two hose clips) and inspect the valves. Most seacocks are not touched from one year to the next, but you must be able to close them immediately if a hose splits or becomes detached. Clean and grease them to be sure that they open and close smoothly. A squirt of WD40 from the outside may help.

# FITTING OUT

The great advantage of sailing through the winter – even if only infrequently – is that there is no need to lay up, and therefore no need to fit out. Whatever you do, there are some jobs that can't – and must not – be avoided.

## Mast and rigging
See above under laying up.

## Topsides
Pride in your boat's appearance will encourage you to give the topsides a good polish, but this is important for other reasons. First, it gives you a good opportunity to inspect the gel coat for any scratches. Unless they are very superficial, they should be filled to prevent further damage. Secondly, it will greatly preserve the value of the boat. Topsides that have been neglected for too long lose their shine and it may be well-nigh impossible to restore without huge effort or by resorting to paint – best avoided if at all possible.

There are some excellent, and very expensive, 'marine' products on the market, but good-quality household or car cleaners and polishes can be just as good.

## Hull below waterline
Beware of a build-up of antifouling. Not only will it add unnecessary weight (a surprising amount over a few years), it will eventually start to part company with the hull and you will be left with an underwater moonscape. A rough underwater surface will slow you down significantly. Even a half a knot reduction means an hour added to a cross-Channel passage.

Rub down the old antifouling as much as possible (wear suitable clothing, mask etc) to reduce a build-up. Most paint manufacturers recommend two coats (I wonder why) but one is usually sufficient unless you sail in an area where there is exceptional fouling.

After several years it may be necessary to remove the whole lot and start again. This can be done by scraping (slow and tedious), with chemicals (messy) or by grit blasting (messy and expensive). There is no easy way, but it does need doing at some

*First sail of the year in calm conditions.*

time. When the old paint has been removed, inspect the hull very closely for signs of osmosis or damage. It may be wise to re-epoxy before antifouling. A surveyor will be able to advise on this, and will almost certainly recommend checking the hull for moisture content before you do so. GRP is slightly porous and moisture can build up over time. A moisture check is quick and simple, and will alert you to impending problems. Around skin fittings and the rudder are common areas for higher than usual moisture readings. It is rare for a modern boat (less than 20 to 30 years old) to develop osmosis, but it is not unknown. Full treatment, when necessary, involves removing the old gel coat and starting again. This is very expensive and time-consuming.

## Underwater fittings

Have a look at all the through-hull fittings and scrape away any muck or excessive paint that has accumulated. Use a long screwdriver or stout wire to delve into the darker recesses.

Pay particular attention to the echo sounder transducer. Its accuracy will be affected by any build-up of paint, so gently rub it down and apply the bare minimum of antifouling.

# ANODES

Anodes should be changed when they have wasted to about 50% of their original size. These anodes have partially corroded and so they are clearly doing their job. Assuming they are only a year old, they should be perfectly serviceable for another season.

However, if it had corroded significantly more than this in just one year, it would be sensible to renew it now.

Be sure to thoroughly clean the hull fittings to ensure good electrical contact, and never paint the anode itself.

*Anode,* BELOW: *Prop anode.*

## Rudder

Give the rudder a good tug to check the bearings. Some movement is acceptable, but get advice if it seems to be excessive.

## Stern gear

No one seems to be able to agree on how to protect the propeller from fouling. Some apply antifouling paint; some use grease; others smear it with special gel; some leave it well alone in the hope that regular use will keep the barnacles at bay. After more than 35 years of owning yachts, I still don't know. One thing is certain: a badly fouled propeller will be much less efficient and you could easily lose speed of a knot or two by the end of the summer. It may be worthwhile having the boat lifted for a quick scrub during the season.

If you have a sail-drive, its oil can only be changed when the boat is out of the water, but it doesn't need changing every year. If the oil (as seen on the dipstick) looks grey or milky, however, something is not right. It probably needs changing or it might indicate worn seals on the bottom of the drive unit. Again, take professional advice.

## Anodes

Sacrificial anodes prevent a multitude of corrosion problems and must be carefully monitored. Most will last a few years but others may need replacing every year. It is a simple job and well worth doing if in any doubt.

Having fitted out, and with the boat back in her natural element, take time to check everything before setting sail. Spend a few hours in calm waters and gentle winds to adjust the rigging, tweak the sails and generally establish your confidence that all is well.

12

# NAVIGATION

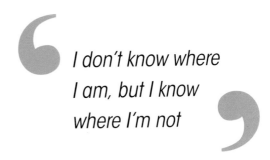

*I don't know where I am, but I know where I'm not*

The quotation above is one of my favourites. Most of the time you don't need to know your exact geographical position, but you do need to know that you are in safe water and not standing into danger. The most obvious way of achieving this in coastal waters is to monitor clearing bearings or sail outside a certain depth contour, say 5m.

This chapter does not attempt to teach you to navigate your yacht – that is already assumed, although I have added a few navigational 'wrinkles' at the end.

As this is your own yacht you can pick and choose your navigational equipment – instruments, publications, electronic aids – rather than making do with what someone else has provided for you. Generally, I have not recommended specific manufacturers, but I have not been able to resist the temptation to identify some of my favourite books and publications. Your boat may have come with a certain amount of navigational gear, some of which will be difficult and expensive to replace. However, I hope you will find the following useful when contemplating changes in the future.

A note of caution: I am a great enthusiast for electronic navigation but not at the expense of more traditional backups. It is very tempting to rely on such wonderful kit as iPads, laptops, chart plotters, AIS and the rest, and to do away with paper charts, books, pencils and dividers. Be very wary of doing so. In a large ship with

*The author pretending to be hard at work.*

duplicated systems and a guaranteed power supply, it is perfectly acceptable (and legal) to leave the charts ashore. A yacht is a different beast altogether. Power supplies do fail, opportunities for charging iPads and laptops may be few and far between, and delicate electronics are very susceptible to damp and the lively motion of a small craft.

You must, therefore, not only carry on board the means of navigating safely if you lose, say, the GPS signal, but also have the knowledge and experience to do so. It is surprising how quickly you can become navigationally rusty without practice, so occasionally turn off or cover up the chart plotter, GPS display and radar and go back to basics. It will help to keep your hand in – and you will have fun!

## INSTRUMENTS

If I had to select just two instruments they would be a compass and an echo sounder. But first let's look at what else you need for basic navigation:

■ **Dividers**

They come in many shapes and sizes, and are essential for measuring distances and plotting positions.

■ **Pair of compasses**

Useful for plotting ranges (from a radar), but the dividers can be used instead.

■ **Pencils**

Always use a soft (2B) pencil on the chart as it is much easier to clean off after use.

■ **Pens**

A ballpoint pen for writing notes and filling in the logbook; coloured non-permanent felt tip pens for use on the plastic covers of Leisure Folios (see below). They can also be used on a radar screen for plotting contacts.

■ **Eraser (rubber)**

For cleaning paper charts after use.

■ **Plotter**

There are many on the market but I favour the Breton (or Portland) plotter, which has a rotatable compass rose in the middle. It is large enough for normal use and a lot less fiddly than parallel rulers.

■ **Clock**

A quartz wristwatch is fine but it is useful to have a small clock at the chart table, which avoids having to roll up wet oilskin sleeves to note the time.

■ **Barometer**

A barometer does not need to be particularly accurate; it is changes in pressure that are important. An inexpensive analogue or battery-powered digital barometer will show pressure trends precisely enough. A rapid rise or fall in pressure of more than 6 millibars in three hours warns that gales are close.

Steady pressure usually means more of the same, while a rising barometer generally heralds fine weather. More details are in *Reeds Weather Handbook*.

■ **Kitchen timer**

This can be used for myriad purposes: reminders to write up the log; warning of impending weather forecasts; plotting at set intervals on a radar screen; indicating when the spuds are cooked.

■ **Hand bearing compass**

The ubiquitous hand bearing compass in a thick rubber 'tyre' is best. It is astonishingly accurate and can withstand the rough and tumble of a small craft at sea. Like the main steering compass, it needs to be swung (checked) at intervals to establish any deviation (see below).

■ **Binoculars**

Although not really an instrument, this is as good a place as any to mention binoculars. First, they are a vital piece of equipment in a yacht, for very obvious reasons. Secondly, the market is awash with them, giving you almost unlimited choice. A pair of 7x50 binoculars is probably ideal (the 7 refers to the magnification, the 50 to the diameter of the objective lens). Binoculars of any higher magnification are almost impossible to hold steadily at sea.

Always try out binoculars before you buy them to be sure they feel right, are easy to use and give a good clear image with no distortion. They will be subjected to a rough life on board and will get wet, so go for robust, rubber-coated ones. There is no need to spend a fortune, but you do get – in optical terms, at least – what you pay for.

A kitchen timer is useful for remembering the shipping forecast or timing the potatoes.

> *Always try out binoculars before you buy them*

## PUBLICATIONS

Go to any good chandlery and you will be spoilt for choice. Here are some of the charts, books and publications that I have found to be useful, reliable and user-friendly.

### Charts

Full-size charts don't fit easily on a yacht's chart table, so you may wish to buy Admiralty Leisure Folios or Imray Chart Packs. These are excellent value and come in plastic covers that can be used for plotting fixes with felt tip pens. They cover almost the whole of the UK, Channel Islands and much of Ireland, but you will need additional, large charts if you are venturing further afield.

Which you choose is a personal choice. The information on both Admiralty and Imray charts is clear and accurate but colouring and layout vary. There are, of course, other publishers, notably the French SHOM (**S**ervice **H**ydrographique et **O**céanographique de la **M**arine), which produces first-rate charts.

Charts need to be kept up to date. Corrections (Notices to Mariners (NTMs)) are available online from the UKHO website. The task is not onerous if you select just those corrections that affect you. You will probably not be interested in a minor change of depth in the middle of the Irish Sea, but you will certainly need to note if a buoy has been moved or a light's characteristics changed. Leisure Folios are not specifically covered by NTMs but they can be kept up to date from their 'source charts'. Each new edition is fully corrected when it goes to print, and new editions are produced every few years.

## Reeds

*Reeds* (and its monthly updates) is an excellent source for general amendments, many of which are based on NTMs, but the chartlets are not designed to be used for navigation – they are merely representations of the area they cover. They are regularly amended but do not claim to be substitutes for official charts.

## Almanacs

The 'Yachtsman's Bible', *Reeds*, lives up to its name and covers the whole of the UK, Ireland, Channel Islands and the continental coasts from the Baltic to Gibraltar, the Azores and Madeira. It is a ready source of information for almost all your passage-planning requirements. If what you need is not there, there is an indication of where to find it. It is rather bulky so you may find one of the regional almanacs more convenient. These have all the same navigational information as the big book but some of the other data is much abridged.

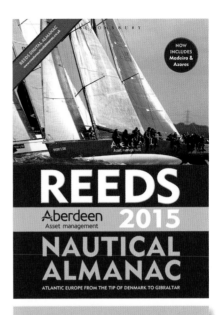

*Reeds Nautical Almanac, 'The Yachtsman's Bible'.*

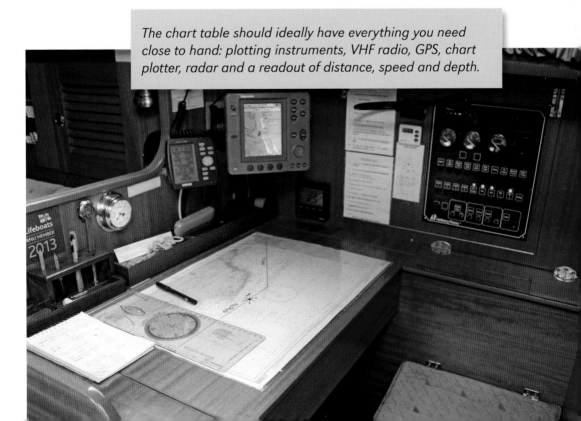

*The chart table should ideally have everything you need close to hand: plotting instruments, VHF radio, GPS, chart plotter, radar and a readout of distance, speed and depth.*

*Reeds* is also available in loose leaf format, or the digital version can be downloaded onto a desktop computer or laptop. *Reeds* iPad version is also available from the iStore. There are other almanacs but I don't know of any that match *Reeds* for reliability and accuracy. However, if your sailing activities are restricted to your local area, the *PBO Small Craft Almanac* may suffice, but be aware that, unlike *Reeds*, it does not have harbour charts.

## Pilots

Otherwise known as *Sailing Directions* or *Cruising Companions*, these provide more subjective detail than most almanacs, which are, by their nature, objective. In pilots you will find further guidance on passages, assessments of facilities in ports and harbours, and advice on shopping, eating and drinking ashore. In other words, pilots complement rather than supplant an almanac. The information in a pilot is generally useable for some time, whereas an almanac is more dynamic, with much data being valid for just the current year.

Rather than give advice on specific pilots, I suggest you have a browse and choose the ones whose styles and content suit you best. Many of them are republished as new editions, so check that you are buying the latest version. You will probably need several depending on your cruising area.

## Tidal stream atlases

*Reeds*, and other almanacs, include tidal stream diagrams but, while they are perfectly adequate for planning purposes, they do tend to be rather too small for accurate navigational use. I don't think you can beat the *Admiralty Tidal Stream Atlases* for accuracy and clarity. Have a look, also, at some of the downloadable tidal apps for tablets. 'TidesPlanner' is particularly good. For the reasons stated already, I would not rely on them as my only source, but they are unquestionably convenient and very good value.

*Yachts in light wind.*

## Logbook

This is an essential 'publication' (see Chapter 3). Although there are many on chandlers' book shelves, I have never been entirely happy with their layout or detail – there is either too much or too little. Some are loose-leaf so you can add more pages when required; bound logbooks usually run out just before the end of your cruise.

Consider carefully what you want to record. A logbook's primary purpose is to note navigational data and weather forecasts, but it is also a record of your sailing activities, so make sure there is plenty of space for remarks. I have kept all my logs since I bought my first yacht in 1979 when an overnight berth in a good marina was expensive at £5!

## Notebook

This is as obvious as it is essential – for recording fixes, noting log readings, copying radio messages, shopping lists and much more. The best are the reporters' notebooks with spiral binding and perforated pages. If you shop around you can buy them in packs of four or five. You can't have too many.

## Miscellaneous books

With suitable charts, tidal stream atlases, pilots and a good almanac you are well set up for all navigational purposes, but you still need some other reference books including:

■ **User manuals**
Keep them handy. When you want to check how to adjust the instrument lights, recalibrate the echo sounder or remind yourself how to switch the radar from north-up to head-up, you don't want to delve into a dark locker to find the right book.

■ **IRPCS (ColRegs)**
It is always useful to have a copy of the ColRegs available, if only to check on the more obscure light and sound signals. Whenever you have a few spare moments, have a look through it to remind yourself of the fundamentals.

If fog is forecast, turn up Rule 19 – probably the least understood rule in the book.

■ **OS maps**
Yachting is not all about sailing; an OS map is your chart for a good walk ashore.

# ELECTRONICS

You can spend a fortune on electronic gizmos. Some are now considered almost indispensible; others are nice to have but by no means essential. In this section I am not including such things as laptops, smartphones, iPads and other tablets. They all have their uses, and some of the programs and apps are astonishingly good value (many are free). It is perfectly possible to have all your navigational data (tides, tidal streams, charts, almanacs etc) on one device – and to lose it all at a stroke if the battery runs low, it gets wet or someone sits on it. Great for planning purposes and perhaps as a backup, but not so good for practical use at sea.

So, let's have a look at fixed items. I have listed them in the very rough order that I think reflects their value in a yacht, but this will be greatly influenced by your boat, your sailing area, how far and how often you sail offshore, and your budget. They all use electricity, so think about the overall power consumption when they are all running. Radar is particularly power hungry when it is transmitting.

# Echo sounder

Often known as a depth sounder, this is the most valuable of all electronic instruments – the nearest point of land is invariably straight down! Not only will it give you warning of imminent grounding in shallow water, it is also an essential aid to navigation. In many areas, and especially when approaching the coast, the echo sounder can provide a much-needed position line as you cross charted depth contours.

An echo sounder will almost certainly be included in the yacht's inventory, so you will be spared the necessity of choosing, buying and fitting one. However, I have included it here to remind you to calibrate it. As you are most likely to depend on it to prevent grounding, it is best calibrated in shallow water by comparing its read-out with the actual depth measured by a lead line (or any line with a weight on the end). Most echo sounders are easily adjusted to show depths in fathoms, feet or metres.

You will also have the option of having the depth shown from the waterline or from below the keel. My advice is the former. A good skipper should always know the approximate height of tide at any time in order to be able to relate the actual depth (by echo sounder) to that shown on the chart. A significant discrepancy probably means you are not where you think you are. In shoal waters it is a simple matter of subtracting your draft from the recorded depth to determine how much water you have under the keel.

Put a note on the display to show where depths are measured from ('depths from the waterline' or 'depths from the keel'). If you don't, you may be in for a nasty surprise when the display shows 1.5 metres (your draft) and you wrongly think it is displaying the depth below the keel.

# Log

Like the echo sounder, you are unlikely to have to fit one yourself. Also like the echo sounder, the log must be calibrated. The easiest way of doing this is to motor at a steady speed in still water (ie, no tidal stream or current). You then just compare the log read-out with the speed over the ground (SOG) from the GPS, making adjustments as necessary. It is important to do this as the log's output will probably feed into a chart plotter and/or radar. You can also motor along one of the many measured miles around the coast. This takes longer and, if there is any stream running, you need to time yourself over at least two runs.

Irritatingly, log impellers are prone to fouling and need to be cleaned. Be sure to do this regularly; don't wait until it stops working. It can be a rather wet and messy job, so train one of your crew to do it for you! If all goes well, not much water will come inboard, but even so I am wary of cleaning the log when underway – just in case.

## VHF radio

The chances are that your boat will already have a VHF radio fitted. If it does not support Digital Selective Calling (DSC), change it for a new one as soon as you can. A DSC radio should have an input from the GPS so that it automatically transmits your current position with a Distress or Urgency call.

Many people regard DSC merely as a means of making emergency transmissions; its role in making Routine calls is sadly misunderstood and therefore underused. If everyone initiated their routine ship-to-ship calls using DSC the incessant traffic on Ch16 would dramatically reduce and life would be much more peaceful. Have a look in the radio's instruction manual and encourage your friends to do the same.

While on the subject of unnecessary transmissions, it is really necessary to conduct a radio check every time you go sailing? I think not, except, perhaps, if you have a newly installed radio or you have had work done on the aerial run. Otherwise, so long as the set is receiving, there is a fighting chance that it will transmit when you want it to. In any case, just because it works during a radio check is no guarantee that it will do so the next time you use it. Modern sets are so reliable and robust that the chances of a failure are very small. If you must make a radio check, try to avoid Ch16. Instead of calling the Coastguard, call a friend on an agreed working channel or by DSC, or a marina office on Ch80.

*A VHF DSC radio is essential for calling for help, but be wary of making unnecessary transmissions on Ch16 for radio checks!*

The main radio is usually sited at the chart table and may be difficult to hear from the cockpit. If the volume is turned up too far it is an irritant for anyone below, especially at night. The solution is to fit a waterproof loudspeaker that can be heard on deck. Most, if not all, radios have a loudspeaker socket so fitting an extension speaker is easy. To operate a VHF radio legally, you must have a Ship Radio Licence (be sure to inform Ofcom that the yacht's ownership has changed) and an Authority to Operate. The latter is personal to you and will usually be in the form of a Short Range Certificate (SRC) for VHF/DSC. Both documents must be kept on board.

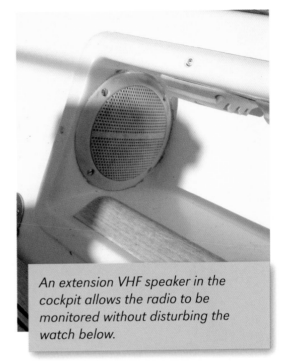

*An extension VHF speaker in the cockpit allows the radio to be monitored without disturbing the watch below.*

## Handheld VHF radio

This is a useful addition to the fixed set. In a fully crewed yacht it may not be difficult to nip below to answer the radio or arrange your overnight berth. If you are short-handed, a handheld radio within reach of the wheel/tiller makes life so much easier. It can also be taken with you in the liferaft – just remember to keep it well charged.

## Radar

For anyone who regularly sails offshore, radar falls into the 'almost essential' category. Many years ago we were caught out in fog (once again) in the middle of the Channel, and the sight of our small children peering anxiously into the gloom persuaded me to fit a radar. Relatively basic sets are not cripplingly expensive and, in the absence of budgetary

*A handheld radio could be invaluable if ever you have to take to the liferaft. Keep it fully charged.*

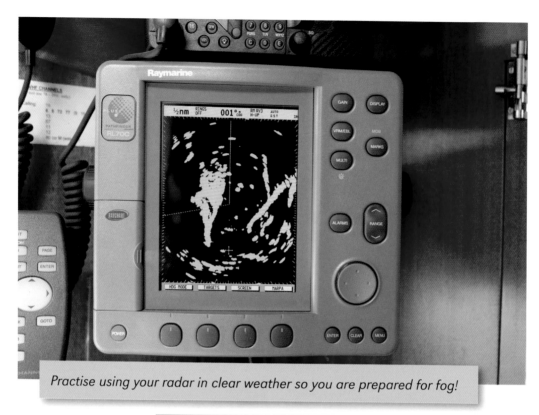

*Practise using your radar in clear weather so you are prepared for fog!*

*Mounting the radar aerial on a pole is relatively inexpensive, although maximum range may be reduced.*

constraints, the mast is probably the ideal position for the aerial. Much easier and less costly is to fit it on a pole at the stern, albeit with some loss of range because it is lower down. With this arrangement, the radome is easier to reach and running the cables is far simpler.

The choice is overwhelming and what you buy will probably be determined by cost. However, think what you need it for: probably the occasional use in fog for collision avoidance and, even more occasionally, for fixing your position. In practice, you are unlikely to use it very much – and that's a problem in itself.

'Radar-assisted collisions' arise, usually, because the operator doesn't know how to interpret the picture or is out of practice. If this strikes a bell with you, enrol on a shore-based course then practise with your own set. In good visibility, with a competent person looking out, try plotting multiple contacts and working out their closest points of approach. At the same time, think what actions you would take to avoid a close-quarters situation if you really were in fog. It's good for you, and it's fun. Play with the controls and find out what the set can do for you. A well-tuned radar in a flat sea should have no difficulty in picking up very small objects, even seagulls.

With GPS constantly telling you exactly where you are, there may not seem to be much requirement to use radar for navigation, but it can be a comforting check, particularly if the picture can be overlaid onto the chart plotter display. In this way, non-charted contacts can be quickly and positively identified as other vessels.

## GPS
GPS has revolutionised navigation. If you are buying a GPS set, consider what it will be linked to: almost certainly a chart plotter and a DSC radio, and possibly a radar display. Some makes are made for each other, and may be designed for a particular chart system. If you are starting from scratch it is advisable to look at the whole package and get everything to match. That is not to say that different brands won't work perfectly well together. Your choice.

Assuming the GPS signal is available – it is easily jammed, so don't rely on it – the most vulnerable item is the aerial, which is usually mounted on the pushpit and is therefore vulnerable to being knocked, grabbed or snagged. A second, basic, GPS aerial and display, which is wired independently of anything else, will at least give you a position if the main one is out of action. Even the most inexpensive models (less than £200) have many of the features of their more sophisticated cousins.

While you are thinking of GPS, a waterproof handheld set, popular with hikers, is well worth considering for emergency use. They are available for less than £100.

*GPS aerials should be mounted low down where movement is minimised.*

## Chart plotter

As ever, there is a huge choice; see my comments under Radar and GPS above. Different makes may only support certain electronic chart systems (C-Map, Navionics et al), and these will be in either raster or vector format. A detailed explanation of these formats is outside the scope of this book, but raster charts are basically copies of paper charts while vector charts are 'layered', allowing more detail to be shown as you zoom in. You may wish to decide on the type of charts you want before looking at chart plotters that support them.

## Autopilot

Autopilots are made for both wheel- and tiller-steered yachts. If you always sail with a full crew, an autopilot may not be high on your list. If you sail short- or single-handed, it is a real bonus for long passages as it leaves you free to look out, adjust the sails or put the kettle on. The great advantage is that it doesn't get bored and will probably steer a more accurate course than even the best helmsman in reasonable conditions but don't rely on it to prevent a crash gybe when sailing downwind in big seas. The only disadvantages are that it can't see where it is going, it can't spot debris in the water, and it won't avoid other vessels.

*An autopilot is useful on long passages or when sailing short-handed.*

Some autopilots can be linked to the GPS/chart plotter so that they maintain track and alter course as you reach the waypoints on your route. Neither of these actions are good practice. First, maintaining a track over a long distance is often less efficient than allowing the boat to be set one way and then the other by the tidal stream. See *Your First Channel Crossing* for more details. Secondly, you will become lazy! Allowing your yacht to 'drive' herself along a predetermined route will inevitably mean that you keep a less efficient lookout, and you must always determine that a new course is safe – from shipping and navigationally – before making an alteration.

The most basic autopilots for a tiller have their own built-in compasses and are thus independent of all electrical inputs other than a 12v power source. More sophisticated versions receive their heading data from another compass (a fixed fluxgate compass, for example).

We use ours for long passages and when I am sailing by myself – especially useful at slow speed while sorting out ropes and fenders before arriving alongside. I am always very aware that if I should fall over the side with the autopilot engaged, the yacht will sail very happily over the horizon. Not a happy thought, so I am careful to be clipped on at all times.

## AIS

AIS (**A**utomatic **I**dentification **S**ystem) is becoming more popular and is now widely fitted in yachts. There is no doubt that it can be invaluable in assisting in collision avoidance, particularly in poor visibility, as it will tell you other ships' names, positions, courses, speeds and more. However, it is not a radar, despite what some manufacturers' advertisements may imply. Also, the use of AIS is not yet included in the Colregs, so you may not have a good case if you are involved in a collision and it is subsequently shown that you were relying on AIS for collision avoidance.

Generally, only vessels over 300GRT are required by SOLAS to have AIS. It is dependent to some extent on user inputs (even if it is fitted, it may not be turned on), and only the strongest signals may be shown in busy areas. In other words, the absence of an AIS target does not mean that there is nothing there! That said, and if the limitations of the system are fully appreciated, AIS is well worth considering. You will need to modify your VHF aerial run or add a separate one.

## NAVTEX

Navtex is a prime method of disseminating Maritime Safety Information (MSI), and is particularly useful for receiving weather forecasts when you are unable to receive VHF broadcasts from shore stations. It is independent of other systems on board, and has its own aerial, receiver and display (or paper printout). Its coverage extends to 270 miles offshore. If you sail mainly in coastal waters with the occasional foray to the Continent, Navtex may not be for you, but it does negate the necessity to remember to turn on the radio to listen to MSI broadcasts.

## Wind instruments

I have put this last as the absence of a wind instrument is not going to stop you sailing. Displays of wind speed and direction are certainly nice to have and can make steering by the wind easier for novices, but they are in no way essential unless you are a racing type who changes sails at exact specified wind speeds. That said, most yachts will have wind instruments already fitted. If not, do you really want to run cables to the top of the mast, install an anemometer and fit the displays? Probably not, but wireless systems are available and may be worth a look.

## Lights

Lights have a section of their own because it is incredible how often you see yachts displaying the wrong ones. Most yachts are fitted with the following navigation lights:

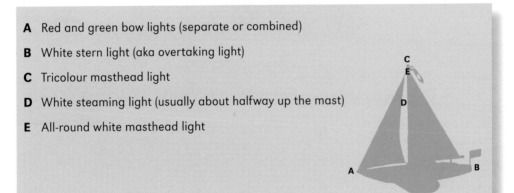

**A**  Red and green bow lights (separate or combined)

**B**  White stern light (aka overtaking light)

**C**  Tricolour masthead light

**D**  White steaming light (usually about halfway up the mast)

**E**  All-round white masthead light

When **sailing** (engine not running) you should show either **A** + **B** or just **C** (not both). When **under power** you should show either **A** + **B** + **D** or **A** + **E** (not **C**).

If you are in crowded waters such as the Thames Estuary or the Solent, big ships will probably see your lights more easily if you show the ones lower down. In other words, when sailing avoid the tricolour (**C**) and use the bow and stern lights (**A** and **B**). At all times when underway, try not to show any other lights that may be confused with any of the above.

When at **anchor** show the white masthead light (**E**) or, much better, any all-round white light lower down where it is more likely to be in the line of sight of other yachts underway in the vicinity. I use an oil lamp secured to the genoa sheets. One tank of oil lasts all night and there is no drain on the batteries. An LED camping lantern is just as effective and uses very little power.

The rules for yachts over 20m LOA are slightly different, so have a look at the Colregs to make sure you get it right.

## Compass

In your own boat you will want to be sure your compass is as accurate as possible. Without wishing to teach you to suck eggs, a compass is affected by changes in direction of the earth's magnetic field (variation) and ferrous bits and pieces in the boat (deviation). Between them they make up the total compass error. Variation can be found from the chart or in an almanac. Along the south coast of England it is only 1° to 2° but off the north-west of Ireland, for example, it is currently about 6°.

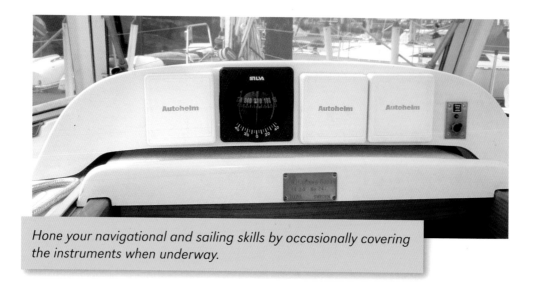

*Hone your navigational and sailing skills by occasionally covering the instruments when underway.*

This is not to be ignored lightly, and due allowance must be made. A combination of both types of errors can easily be 10° or more.

Deviation varies according to heading and has to be established by 'swinging the compass'. To be pedantic, the term 'swinging the compass' involves checking for errors, adjusting the compass to minimise them, then drawing up a table showing the residual errors. In practice you need to just check the compass on various headings and make a note (or draw a table) of errors of more than a degree or so (most small boat compasses are graduated in increments of 5°).

There are a couple of simple ways of doing this. Make sure that there are no loose magnetic objects near the compass – portable radios, torches and mobile phones are obvious culprits.

### Visual bearings

Fix your position as accurately as possible but well clear of any ferrous objects. Close alongside a large navigation buoy is not a good choice, but close to a wooden pile may be. Alternatively, establish your position by transits, bearings, radar or, best, GPS.

> *A useful mnemonic is CADET: **C**ompass **AD**d **E**ast to get **T**rue*

From there, and being careful not to move too far from your position, turn the boat to point directly at charted objects – which, for accuracy, should be as far away as possible – and note the heading by the steering compass (and the autopilot compass if relevant). At the same time take a bearing with the hand bearing compass, then compare the readings with the magnetic bearing from the chart. Do this on as many headings as possible; every 15° is ideal, but every 30° will usually be quite adequate.

### GPS

With no crosstide, preferably slack water, motor on a steady compass heading and compare that with course over the ground (COG) as shown by the GPS. Make sure it is displaying magnetic, not true, readings. To check the hand bearing compass, take a bearing of the forestay or any object that is dead ahead. Again, do this on several headings.

Having found any deviation, draw up a table showing its values, east or west, on various headings. The next job it to apply it, along with variation, for your particular heading. As a reminder, easterly variation/deviation is added to obtain true headings; westerly errors are subtracted.

## Sketches

Get into the habit of making a sketch of pilotage passages in a notebook. Keep it simple but show navigational marks, your intended track and any other information you need. This saves constant trips to the chart table as it is rarely a good idea to have a chart in the cockpit where it can get wet (if not in a waterproof sleeve) or blow away.

## Confusing miles

There are many different miles: statute, nautical, sea, geographical and data, to name just five. Although the term Nautical Mile (NM) is often used, the strictly correct unit of distance at sea is the Sea Mile. It varies from about 1843 metres at the equator to about 1862 metres at the poles. An NM is defined as 1852 metres. Check the settings on your chart plotter, iPad etc as there is usually an option to select different units of distance.

Remember that, due to the way the surface of the earth is projected onto a flat chart, the length of a mile shown on the chart varies with latitude. On large-scale charts this makes little practical difference, but at smaller scales – such as charts of the North Sea or Irish Sea – quite significant errors can be introduced if you use the scale towards the bottom of the chart to measure distances near the top.

# WRINKLES (HINTS AND TIPS)

You will find a plethora of navigational hints and tips in books dedicated to the subject. Here are a few that you may find useful.

## ✦ Passage planning

It is a requirement under the International Convention for Safety of Life at Sea (SOLAS) that all passages beyond sheltered waters must be planned. Although the plan does not have to be recorded on paper, in the event of legal action following an incident a written plan would be clear proof that the appropriate planning had been completed. The Solent is considered to be sheltered; the English Channel is not. This Passage Planning Form [in the Appendix], when completed, would satisfy that requirement. You don't need to fill in every part for every passage, but weather forecasts, tides and dangers (if any) are clearly necessary. The form may be copied or modified to suit your needs. There is a similar form in *Reeds*.

## ✦ Tidal coefficients

These are shown in *Reeds* and indicate the magnitude of the tide on any particular day without having to look up and calculate the range to determine whether it is springs, neaps or somewhere in between. Access times for many French ports are defined by the tidal coefficient related to your draft. A coefficient of 95 indicates a mean spring tide; 70 an average tide; 45 a mean neap tide.

## ✦ Six-minute rule

Six minutes is a tenth of an hour so in that time you will travel through the water a tenth of your speed in miles. At 5 knots, therefore, you will travel 0·5 miles. In three minutes you will travel half the distance (0·25 miles); in 12 minutes it will be twice (1 mile). This 'wrinkle' is invaluable when conducting blind pilotage in fog or when plotting a running fix. Remember to take into account any tidal stream.

## ✦ Running fix

When you only have one charted object to fix on – a lighthouse, perhaps – take a bearing of it and plot the position line on the chart, noting the log reading and the time. A few minutes later repeat the process. Now transfer the first position line by the distance and course you have made good over the ground between the two bearings, remembering to include allowance for any tidal stream. Where the lines cross is where you were at the time of the second bearing. Simple but effective.

### ✦ Course to steer

Always order a course to steer that ends in a 0 or 5. If you order 147°, the helmsman will steer about 145° anyhow! The important thing is to make sure the helmsman tells you what course he/she has actually steered, on average, at the end of his trick. This is the course you should use for working up your DR/EP.

If you need to give a course to steer in a hurry, give it to the nearest 10° or so (or even just, 'south-west'), then work it out more accurately.

*'There are no decimal points in snap headings'*

### ✦ Distance off track

This is easily calculated by knowing that a 1° difference in bearing between two objects 6 miles away indicates that they are 1 cable (0·1 mile) apart. A 5° compass error over 60 miles will therefore see you 5 miles off track.

### ✦ Dutchman's log

This is useful if your main log is not working – because of weed round the impeller, perhaps. Time how long it takes an object (piece of paper, apple core – it doesn't matter) dropped at the bows to reach the stern.

Speed (knots) = (LOA x 0·592) ÷ time (seconds).
So, for a 34ft boat and a time of 5 seconds,
the speed is 34 x 0·592 ÷ 5 = 4 knots.

You can draw up a table of time and speed for your own yacht.

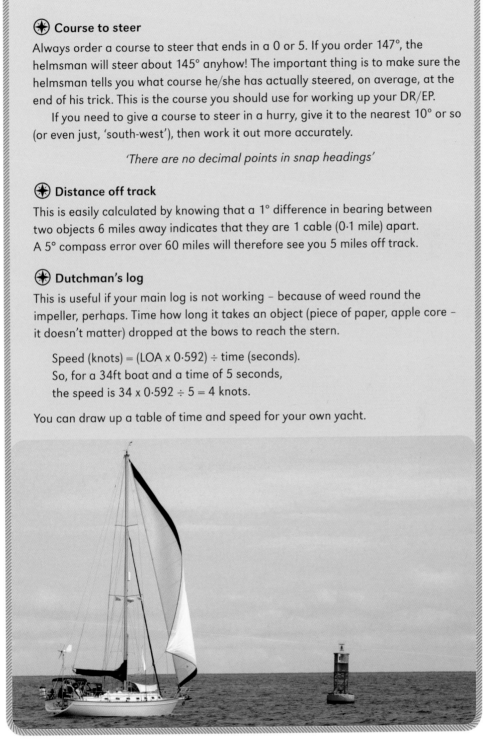

# SAFETY

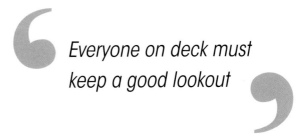

*Everyone on deck must keep a good lookout*

No book about boats and sailing can be complete without a few words on safety. I have no intention of reiterating all the training, experience and advice you have mustered so far, but safety must be every skipper's number one priority. There is excellent guidance in *Reeds* and elsewhere about what safety gear you should carry. This section aims to expand on the choice and use of some of it. Safety is your responsibility, and you must decide what best suits you, your boat and your crew. You make the rules, and you must ensure that they are obeyed.

The three most obvious hazards in any vessel are fire, flood and someone falling over the side (MOB). Of these, by far the most frightening is fire. A flood is quite likely to be containable unless the hull is severely breached (for example, by a collision), and you should be well practised at picking up an MOB. The latter is, of course, a potentially perilous situation and may justify a MAYDAY call, but a fire that is not brought under control immediately can spread very rapidly, probably leaving no escape except for the liferaft.

Unless you allow smoking below decks (don't!), the main sources of fire are the galley and the engine. You may decide to forbid open-pan frying while underway, and you should certainly ensure that all matches are dunked in water or under a tap before being put in the gash bin.

As for the engine, good maintenance and a clean engine compartment are the keys to fire prevention. Any hint of overheating or any sign of smoke must be investigated without delay, but beware of opening the engine box if you suspect an actual fire. The more air you introduce, the more likelihood of the fire developing. If in doubt, shut down the engine, isolate the fuel if possible and then monitor the situation carefully. A fire on board will almost invariably warrant a PAN PAN or MAYDAY call.

It is all very well having the right kit on board but it is of no use at all unless it is fully serviceable and everyone knows how to use it. The only SOLAS requirements for small private pleasure vessels are to carry a radar reflector ('if practicable') and a copy of the lifesaving signals. The latter may be found in *Reeds* so, if you have a copy on board, you are covered.

## EQUIPMENT – BELOW DECKS

### Fire extinguishers

The Maritime and Coastguard Agency (MCA) and *Reeds* both provide good advice about the number and type of extinguishers that should be carried. When siting them, remember that if they are too close to the fire you may not be able to get at them in an emergency. There is a lot to be said for having at least one extinguisher in the cockpit and another in the forepeak as the fore hatch may be your only access route if the companionway is blocked. Make sure your crew know where they are, how to operate them, and which extinguishers are suitable for different types of fire – oil, gas, electrical etc.

### Fire blanket

Have a fire blanket close to the galley. Once it has been placed over a burning pan, leave it there until you are sure any fire is out.

*Fire extinguishers: know where they are and how to use them.*

# EQUIPMENT – UPPER DECK

## Liferaft

If you normally cruise in local waters in daylight, you may not own or need a liferaft. A dinghy, with oars/paddles, towed astern or inflated and ready to launch at short notice, may be perfectly suitable.

If you cruise further offshore, a liferaft is a vital piece of safety equipment. They are expensive to buy and must be regularly serviced, but it is possible to hire one relatively cheaply for a few weeks at a time. For years I kidded myself that a semi-inflated dinghy on the coach roof would be adequate. Once in the water it would be easy to fully inflate it using the pump that had been carefully secured to one of the lifting strops. In hindsight, I am glad I never had to use it in anger: it simply would not have worked.

Make sure a liferaft, if carried, does not become buried in a cockpit locker. It must be readily available for rapid deployment, and this is particularly pertinent when sailing in fog. Ideally, it should be secured on deck with a hydrostatic release mechanism that allows the raft to float free if the boat sinks. If you hire one, and don't therefore have a permanent fitting for it, make sure you don't lash it down so securely that it can't be released immediately. Relying on a knife to sever cordage is not a sensible option. It is far better to use webbing with quick-release buckles.

If the worst comes to the worst, the aim is to step into the liferaft (or dinghy) without getting wet and dressed in warm waterproof clothing. However, abandoning ship is a last resort; it is invariably safer to remain with the yacht unless she is on fire or actually sinking under you.

## Lifejackets

A lifejacket will turn you face-up in the water; a buoyancy aid will not. The latter are fine for messing about in dinghies but are no substitute for lifejackets in larger vessels. Have at least enough lifejackets for each member of the crew with one or two spare. The best are those with both manual and automatic inflation. They must be checked regularly to ensure that all the fittings are sound, the gas bottle is serviceable and secure, and that they hold their pressure for at least 24 hours. If in any doubt, get professional help.

*It is the skipper's responsibility to decide when lifejackets need not be worn.*

All lifejackets should have crotch straps to prevent them riding up and, ideally, a hood that covers the face. Each member of the crew should be allocated their own lifejacket and should take time to adjust the fittings so it can be donned quickly and easily, over foul-weather gear if necessary.

The RNLI's mantra is 'Useless unless worn'. This is, obviously, quite correct and you should decide when they need not be worn. Apart from non-swimmers – who should wear a lifejacket at all times when afloat – you may like to relax the rules to suit the conditions. At least we still have the option in the UK, thank goodness, of making our own judgement on this. In our boat, for what it is worth, we all wear lifejackets:

- At night
- In fog
- When there are two or more reefs in the mainsail
- In the dinghy except in daylight in totally sheltered waters
- Whenever I feel it is sensible to do so

## Harnesses

A lifejacket will keep you afloat when you fall overboard, but there really is no excuse for doing so. It is so much better to stay with the boat! For this reason, I wear a harness more than I wear a lifejacket. Unless you have separate harnesses, which are lighter and more comfortable than a lifejacket, you will have to use the ones built into your lifejackets anyhow.

To be effective, a harness must, like a lifejacket, be properly adjusted and fit snugly. It must also be secured to the boat. This is achieved by having several strong points in the cockpit – ideally reachable from the main hatchway – and webbing lifelines on deck. Guardrails are not suitable – they are not necessarily strong enough, and the stanchions prevent a clear run from bow to stern. The lifelines should therefore run the whole length of the boat so that you can remain hooked on when moving anywhere between pushpit and pulpit. Anyone venturing forward should hook on before leaving the relative safety of the cockpit.

Don't rig the lifelines too tight. If they are used to hold someone on board, they will be exposed to much less strain if they are relatively slack.

A harness may be less bulky and more comfortable than a lifejacket. However, it is useless unless clipped onto the boat.

The lifelines should not be too taut, but they must be securely attached to the boat. Do not rely on the guard wires.

## Dan buoy

A dan buoy fitted with a bright flag can be vital for locating someone in the water. It must be deployed immediately the person falls over the side, and it must be readily visible. If it is telescopic, as most are, keep it at full stretch as the last thing you want to do in an MOB situation is to waste time extending it. To keep the flag in good condition, fold it inside a cover (a short length of plastic pipe perhaps) that is attached to the backstay. As the dan buoy is thrown over the side, the flag is released.

## Lifebelt

This should be fitted with a light that comes on automatically when it is in the water. A fixed, rather than flashing, light is easier to spot in a choppy sea. A small drogue will stop it drifting too quickly with the wind.

# SAILING AT NIGHT OR IN FOG

I have included a short section here about sailing at night or in fog as they both raise their own safety issues. More details can be found in *Your First Channel Crossing*. If you have not done much night sailing before, you might be a bit apprehensive. As always, preparation is the key.

- Make sure all the crew wear **harnesses** and **lifejackets** (fitted with properly adjusted crotch straps) whenever they come up from below. With everyone clipped on, the cockpit can end up with a bit of a snakes' wedding of safety lines, but don't be tempted to relax this rule as you will be very lucky to find and recover a man overboard in the dark. For that reason anyone going on deck must clip on, preferably to a suitable jackstay, before leaving the cockpit.

- Show the appropriate **navigation lights**, but keep others to a minimum. A cigarette lighter, a bright cabin light or a chart plotter's illumination turned up too high can impair your night vision for up to 20 minutes.

- Have a **torch** to hand that is powerful enough to light up the sails if you are in any doubt about whether another vessel has seen you.

- Have a white 'ship scarer' **flare** available.

- Choose a **sail plan** that needs the minimum of attention. Spinnakers and cruising chutes are not, generally, prudent night-time sails. Some skippers take in a reef in the mainsail and a few rolls in the genoa as a precaution. It depends on the actual and forecast weather, but a slightly shortened foresail will certainly make looking out to leeward a lot easier.

- Everyone on deck must keep a good **lookout**. This is equally applicable by day and is a requirement of the Colregs (Rule 5). Make sure someone ducks down to peer under the foresail at frequent intervals. Also check that a good watch is kept to windward where wind and spray might make this difficult and unpleasant. Fishing gear abounds on both sides of the Channel, and sometimes in the middle, so be prepared to take quick avoiding action if a sharp-eyed lookout spots any. Patches of seaweed often mask other floating hazards such as old rope. Steer round them to be on the safe side.

- Remember that body clocks are at their lowest in the early hours, so keep everyone occupied and ensure a steady supply of **snacks** and **hot drinks**.

- During quiet periods try to get some **rest** yourself. You are unlikely to drop off into a deep sleep but an hour or so lying down, even in full oilskins, will help to keep you alert for when you are needed.

Fog is generally well forecast, and you would be unwise to set off if widespread fog was predicted. A report of 'occasional fog patches' in the shipping forecast, on the other hand, is not necessarily a reason to abandon your trip. Sailing in fog is disorientating and somewhat forbidding; you need to be prepared and take appropriate precautions. These include:

- Put a **fix** on the chart. Fog may envelop you anywhere, but if you are closing land it is essential to refine your position as best you can, and plot it on the chart, before entering an area of poor visibility. Once you are in it, you will have plenty to occupy you.

- Get **everyone on deck** and looking out. You may wish to send someone to the foredeck where they will not be distracted by others or have the noise of the engine to contend with.

- Consider lowering the **spray hood** to give better visibility.

- **Listen** for big ships' engines: they don't always sound fog signals.

- If you have **radar**, the most experienced operator should be on constant watch with clear communications to the helm.

- **AIS** may help identify other ships, but be very cautious about using VHF unless you are absolutely sure you know who you are calling. There may be other small vessels around, and the potential for confusion is enormous. It is far better to obey the Colregs to the letter and do your utmost to avoid any close-quarters situations.

- Wear **lifejackets** but consider not using harnesses in the cockpit. If you are run down, you don't want to be attached to the boat. For those on deck, the difficulty of recovering an MOB in fog possibly outweighs this risk. It is a judgement call for the skipper.

- Turn on appropriate **navigation lights** and, to comply with the Colregs, make sound signals. They won't be heard in a large ship, but may alert other yachts or fishing vessels to your presence.

- If sailing, be able to **manoeuvre** quickly. Spinnakers and boomed-out headsails should not be used in fog.

- Have the **engine** running, or ready to start, so you can take immediate avoiding action if necessary.

- Have the **liferaft** ready to deploy. If you don't carry a liferaft, consider inflating the dinghy and towing it astern.

*Fog clearing. This ship was first sighted less than half a mile away.*

The rules for collision avoidance in poor visibility are very different from those when vessels are in sight of one another. Unlike Rules 11–18, Rule 19 (Conduct of vessels in restricted visibility) makes no distinction between stand-on and give-way vessels; guidance on action to take to avoid collision is quite different, and the usual manoeuvring sound signals do not apply. Rule 19 needs to be read very carefully; parts of it are not immediately obvious, but you really do need to understand it thoroughly. Once you are in fog, you will be far too busy to look it up!

## RAISING THE ALARM

### Flares

There is no requirement to carry flares in private pleasure vessels under 13.7 metres LOA (45ft). Indeed, you are not bound to carry any particular lifesaving apparatus, so whether you carry flares or not is entirely up to you. The only regulation you need to be aware of is that, at the time of writing, the French authorities demand that any flares on board must be in date. So, if you do carry them, be sure that they are in date and accessible, and that you know how to use them. An emergency is no time to start reading the instructions.

*Reeds* provides good guidance on the number and type of flares that should be carried, depending on how far offshore you plan to sail.

## EPIRBs/PLBs

**E**mergency **P**osition **I**ndicating **R**adio **B**eacons (EPIRBs) and **P**ersonal **L**ocator **B**eacons (PLBs) are worth considering if you frequently sail offshore. They have an unlimited range as they communicate via satellites and, if fitted with GPS (most are), they transmit your position automatically. Some skippers quite reasonably consider them to be the modern substitute for flares.

## DSC

For most of us, VHF DSC radio is now the most effective method of summoning help in an emergency. As with any other safety equipment, read the instructions carefully and make sure at least one other member of your crew is familiar with the procedures. The great advantage of DSC is that it only takes one press of the red button to initiate a Distress alert. If you have time, you can programme it to give rather more information – on fire, sinking etc – and input your position if it is not already linked to the GPS.

Have a checklist near to the radio for making Distress (MAYDAY) or Urgency (PAN PAN) voice calls. You may think you know what to say, but in the heat of the moment it is not that simple.

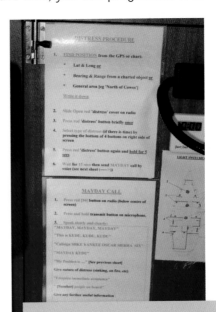

## Mobile phones

The use of mobile phones in an emergency at sea is strongly discouraged. Not only do they bypass the well-established dedicated systems, they have very limited range (typically no more than about 10 miles offshore), they do not 'broadcast' to other vessels that may be in a position to help, and they are very vulnerable to getting wet. That said, when all other means of raising the alarm have failed, mobile phones have saved many lives.

*It is easy to become confused in an emergency. A checklist helps to send a clear distress or urgency message.*

## Handheld GPS/Radio

Having alerted the rescue services (or nearby vessels) of your plight you may have to take to the liferaft. In this case, a handheld GPS and a handheld VHF radio will enable you to update your position and situation. Take spare batteries with you.

# APPENDIX

## PASSAGE PLANNING FORM

DATE: ..................... FROM: ...................... TO: ...................... Dist: ..........nm

Alternative Destination(s):

...................................................................................

Notes:

<u>WEATHER</u> Forecast at:...............................................................................

.............................................................................................................

Forecasts available during passage:

.............................................................................................................

## TIDES

Date: ..........................    Date: .....................    Date: .....................
Place: .............................Place: ...........................   Place: .......................
HW  .............  .........   HW  .............  .........   HW.............  .........
LW  .............  .........   LW  .............  .........   LW.............  .........
HW  .............  .........   HW  .............  .........   HW.............  .........
LW  .............  .........   LW  .............  .........   LW.............  .........
Range: ............. m (.......%)   Range:  ............. m   Range: ...............m

H of T at .............................   .............hrs ...............m
                                         .............hrs ...............m
Depth constraints:

<u>TIDAL STREAMS</u> at .........................................

Turns ....... at ................ Total Set (Fm ............. To .............): .................. ° ....... nm
Turns ....... at ................ Total Set (Fm ............. To .............): .................. ° ....... nm

Net Tidal Stream for Passage: _____ ° _____nm

Estimated Time: ....................Hours  ETD: ......................... ETA: .........................

<u>SUN/MOON</u>     Sunrise: ................... Sunset: ..................
                 Moonrise: ............. Moonset: ................ Phase: ...................

## WAYPOINTS

| No | Name | Course | Distance |
|----|------|--------|----------|
| ....... | ................................. | .................. | .................... |
| ....... | ................................. | .................. | .................... |
| ....... | ................................. | .................. | .................... |
| ....... | ................................. | .................. | .................... |
| ....... | ................................. | .................. | .................... |
| ....... | ................................. | .................. | .................... |

DANGERS                              Clearing Bearings/Ranges/Depths
……..………………………………………………………………………………….
………………………………………………………………………………………….
………………………………………………………………………………...............
…..
………………………………………………………………………………………...
……………………………………………………………………………………….

LIGHTS/MARKS
Expect ……………………………….   at …................…
             …………………………………   at …................…
             …………………………………   at …................…

COMMUNICATIONS
…………………………… (Port/Marina)  Ch………..Telephone ………………………….
…………………………… (Port/Marina)  Ch………..Telephone ……………….………...

NOTES  (Charts prepared & page numbers of relevant pilots/almanacs/etc)

----------------------------------------------------------------------------------------------------------------

## PASSAGE REPORT TO COASTGUARD

This is yacht [Name]

Callsign:  [Callsign in phonetic alphabet]

MMSI number:

On passage from …………………………  to …………………………………

Departing/Departed ……………………………… at ………………………..[**AND/OR**]

My present position is ………………………………………………………………………

ETA at …………………………….  is ………………………………….

……… Adults ………. Children on board

[Name] Coastguard holds my CG66

# FURTHER READING AND WEBSITES

## Other titles of interest

**Your First Channel Crossing**
Planning, Preparing and Executing a
Successful Passage, for Sail and Power
By Andy Du Port
ISBN 978 1 4081 0012 7

**Be Your Own Boat Surveyor**
A hands-on guide for all
owners and buyers
By Dag Pike
ISBN 978 1 4729 0367 9

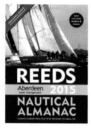

**Reeds Aberdeen Asset Management
Nautical Almanac 2015**
ISBN 978 1 4729 0699 1

**Reeds Weather Handbook**
By Frank Singleton
ISBN 978 1 4081 5247 8

**Reeds PBO Small Craft
Almanac 2015**
ISBN 978 1 4729 1243 5

**The Adlard Coles Maintenance
Logbook for Sail and Power**
By Robert Dearn
ISBN 978 1 4081 7230 8

## Useful websites

Royal Yachting Association (RYA)            www.rya.org.uk
Maritime and Coastguard Agency (MCA)   www.mcga.gov.uk
HM Revenue and Customs (HMRC)          www.gov.uk/mca
Ofcom                                             www.ofcom.org.uk

# INDEX

Key entries are shown in **bold**.